CO|

CW00859782

How to write persuasive sales copy
and build a copywriting business from scratch.

Quentin Pain
United Kingdom

COPY

© Quentin Pain. All rights reserved by the copyright holder including the rights to reproduce this book in any form whatsoever.

All trademarks and registered trademarks mentioned herein are hereby acknowledged and duly recognised as the property of their respective copyright holders and owners and are only mentioned in this text as examples of how phrases and words can be used to further enhance the virtues and features of the companies and products they advertise.

First Edition: March 2021

Designed by Quentin Pain (QuentinPain.com)

1 3 5 7 9 10 8 6 4 2

DISCLAIMER
The author of this book does not offer business advice, just information of a general nature to help you in your quest for business success. This book is not designed to be a definitive guide or to take the place of advice from qualified professionals, and there is no guarantee that the methods suggested in this book will be successful, owing to the risk that is involved in business of every kind. Thus, neither the publisher nor the author assume liability for any losses that may be sustained by the use of the methods described in this book, and any such liability is hereby expressly disclaimed. In the event you use any of the information in this book for yourself, the author and the publisher assume no responsibility for your actions.

DEDICATION

This book is dedicated to all the heroes who wield only the pen to help people achieve their dreams and desires.

To find more information on copywriting, go to:
ScienceOfCopywriting.com

NOTES ON GRAMMAR

Numbers

I sometimes break convention when it comes to numbers. Traditionally, if I were going to write "these 2 lines" I would write "two" instead of "2", however, sometimes it's clearer to use a number instead. For example, I might mention "1 in 10" or "top 10" or "59 character limit".

Punctuation and British English

When it comes to spelling and punctuation, being British, I mostly follow British rules - but not always. For example, I prefer the so-called British logical way to add punctuation within quote marks, but only where it makes sense (to me) to do so. I also sometimes use the $ sign (e.g., for statistics where they have been specified in US dollars) as well as the British pound symbol (£).

Brackets

Sometimes you may see a word or phrase enclosed in [square brackets]. I use square brackets to show placeholder text. Replace this text with something relevant to you or what you're advertising (e.g., in a headline template).

Check first

Whatever choices you make about grammar and style, I highly recommend you ask your clients if they follow any specific style guides before you undertake any work for them. This may save you a great deal of time or embarrassment later on when editing.

Contents

1 The word...

In the beginning was the word...

And the word began with W. We have no idea what the first spoken word was, but there's every chance it had something to do with basic journalism, namely: the who, what, why, where, and when of any story worth listening to.

Following on from that, perhaps the next word was: how. If not, it would soon follow.

Humans, like all animals, are inquisitive by nature. We want to know what's going on, and if it turns out to be of any interest at all, we then want to know what's in it for us (also known as survival, greed, and a whole bunch of other things).

The person who has the answer to these questions automatically becomes the expert and will be sought out by those who need that answer.

But the person who can manipulate those words to stir a desire (even seemingly out of thin air) is the real Master, and that skill is what every copywriter strives for.

There's a problem though. Here's the Google definition of desire: "a strong feeling that you want something." So how do we create a "strong feeling", and how will that lead to a desire to "want something"?

That is what copywriting is. A way to build desire so strong, any product or service will sell itself. This book is here to help you do exactly that.

Copywriters have been arguing forever whether it's possible to create desire from scratch. Most say it's not. But what they really mean is this: "desire is expensive, so don't waste your time trying to create it, instead build on what already exists, that way you'll get more clients with less effort."

This is CRITICAL to your (and your future clients') success. Don't waste your time trying to create desire, instead, BUILD IT - that is, build on what's already there.

There's another lesson too. The lesson of the WORD. Every word matters and every word counts. The more you think about each word, its meaning, and its use, the better your copy will become (not so you become a walking dictionary, but so you become a master of the why, what, and how).

It's not just every word though. It's every sentence, every paragraph, and every piece of copy that makes up a sequence designed to build desire from an audience. It all counts. Bore the pants off people and you lose them. EVERY WORD COUNTS. Remember this if nothing else in your quest to become a great copywriter.

NOTE: In chapter 10 on editing, you'll discover that ALL top writers edit. And then they edit, and edit, and edit again. They are not fearful of editing out some gem of wisdom they may never write again. They know that the more they write and edit, the better their writing becomes. ALWAYS.

If you intend to write in English, but English is not your first language, you're going to need to learn English grammar and English usage. There's no escaping this. The bible is Fowler's English Usage. Study it well, and remember that English is not a particularly logical language.

For example, in the context of copywriting, 'copy' is both a single and plural noun (never say 'copies', that's something entirely different, and never say 'a copy' either, that too means something different and not connected in any way to copy in the context of copywriting, on the other hand, and in certain circumstances, 'the copy' is OK - e.g., "The copy you wrote is rubbish, but I like your style").

What is copywriting?

Copywriting is selling using the printed word. Any piece of writing that encourages someone to buy something is copy. Everything else is content. So always ask the question "what is this trying to sell?" if the answer is 'nothing', then it's not copy, otherwise it is.

Why does that matter? Because copy is worth considerably more than content. And why does being worth more matter? Because value is easier to sell to a prospect. Why does being easier to sell to a prospect matter? Because that's what copywriters do, they sell value using the printed word.

Cause and effect

Read the last two paragraphs again. It's an example of something called First Principles, The First Principles framework is the fastest way to get down to the root cause of anything. And since research is the key to great copy, we are going to need to know how to research everything we do.

Who can be a copywriter?

If you can write, you can be a copywriter. But armed with this book, you'll become a better copywriter than most.

There's a commonly held belief that English is the copywriter's language of choice. That for some reason, there's more money and demand for it. That somehow, English speaking companies have some kind of monopoly when it comes to copywriting.

But the truth is, EVERY country on our planet sells something, and where something is sold, no matter what the language, copywriters are needed. A copywriter who understands this will always sell more to more people more of the time than any other type of writer.

And a good copywriter knows how to get that message across to businesses, no matter where they are in the world.

So if being a copywriter is your passion, vocation, or even hobby, you're in the very best industry there is. Of all the marketing disciplines, copywriting is the top. Without words, there are no sales. That's what we do. And that's how we earn ourselves (and our clients) a decent living.

Money

I just hinted at money. Money drives the consumer market, so it's no wonder most of us are obsessed with it. We have this strongly held belief that without it we are helpless, but once we believe that, it becomes our reality.

As a result, everything we do now hinges on the accumulation of money. We lose focus on why we needed it in the first place. Every expansion we dream of requires even more money to the point that we stop dreaming altogether.

And yet almost every successful entrepreneur who went bankrupt dug themselves out of it (or died trying - very few give up once they've tasted an independent life). So how did they achieve success again starting with nothing? Collaboration.

Whilst in the beginning there was the word - there was no money. It hadn't been invented yet because a medium of exchange wasn't yet needed.

Everything ever invented started with a problem followed by a thought, and the best news for us copywriters is that we translate our thoughts into words, and those words cost nothing (apart from time, a little sweat, and perhaps a few tears).

Now I have your attention, let's focus on that.

2 Attention

Whomever it was that came up with the AIDA acronym got at least one of those letters right: A for Attention. Without attention, we can't sell a bean. That makes it the most important commodity in marketing.

If I have your attention, then I also have your time, and time is the most valuable asset of all. This is why we begin our journey with attention.

Back in the day, the copywriting gods decreed one rule: a headline exists to grab attention and take the reader to the next sentence - usually that means the sub-headline. The sub-headline exists to keep that attention and take our reader to the next sentence. Each sentence exists to build more attention and take our reader onwards to the next paragraph, finally to end up at the call to action in the hope that we've built enough desire and answered enough objections for the reader to buy whatever it is we're trying to sell.

If you remember nothing else about copywriting, remember that last paragraph. Write it out so it sinks in, then stick it somewhere you see every day until it becomes part of your reason to exist.

Doing this will stop you from committing the first deadly sin of copy - writing something no one wants to read - e.g., something boring (it's the fastest way to lose attention).

If you use a complicated word your reader has to look up, you will lose attention. If you use a cliche, your reader will most likely get bored and lose attention (although sometimes a cliche is necessary). If you use a foreign word or phrase your reader doesn't understand, you will lose attention. If you use hyperbole the same will happen ad infinitum (see what I did there? - and see how boring the 'see what I did there?' cliche is too).

This is why I stated so loudly in the introduction that EVERY WORD MATTERS (as does every sentence and paragraph).

What exactly is attention anyway?

Google's dictionary definition is not quite right: "notice taken of someone or something; the regarding of someone or something as interesting or important." There are many important things that are not interesting, and if something is not interesting, it will get ZERO attention.

For ALL animals including humans, attention is anything that catches one of our 5 senses when it's least expecting it - and even then, if it just happens to be a little too different, it may not be picked up at all (i.e., it would get our attention if only we could see, hear, smell, taste, or touch it).

This is called a DISTINCTION. To get attention, something must be distinct from everything else. This is why the following two definitions (both from Google) of the word distinction make sense:

"a difference or contrast between similar things or people" and "excellence that sets someone or something apart from others."

Because, as copywriters, we're using words to get attention, our words can affect all 5 senses. This is a powerful concept to take on board - especially if you've not thought about it before. Remember it well.

How to get attention

Think carefully about which senses you want to agitate. Then think about why you chose those particular senses.

If we're writing some copy for a restaurant, the obvious sense we want to invoke is going to be taste, but taste without some visual reference is akin to blind-tasting, and that rarely works out as expected, so we know we need to invoke both taste and sight as a minimum.

If our copy was to sell children's toys or carpentry tools, taste would be unlikely, but touch would be significant.

What about financial products? A mortgage, for example, has no taste, smell, touch, and it certainly can't be heard, which just leaves us with sight, right? Can you 'see' a mortgage? Not really, but you can certainly see images of the house it will buy, and the signed contract as it drops on the doormat, not to mention the look on your spouse's face as you announce the good news.

The sixth sense

Let me break this gently. There is no sixth sense. There are only synapses in the three nervous systems that run and control our bodies and thoughts. But we'll call that process the sixth sense anyway. Why not! Every label was invented for a reason, and that reason is to explain something we don't understand (life, the universe, and pretty much everything really).

As our 5 senses work to make sense of the world, our synapses fire and our thought processes occur (that's about as much as anyone knows). When it comes to reading copy, we can go a little deeper though.

We start with sight (we visually take in the words). If we're watching a Video Sales Letter (VSL), we're also hearing the words being spoken (this perhaps is why VSLs work so well).

As we see or hear those words, some of them will trigger our other senses. For example, if you were to see a baker removing a loaf of bread from an oven, you'd most likely start to smell the delicious aroma of freshly baked bread and feel the warmth of the oven (and if you didn't, you'd certainly get those things once I'd told you in words what to smell and feel).

Yet we had no external stimulus other than an image. It's therefore easy to fool the brain using our 'sixth sense' (using one or more of our senses to trigger other ones internally).

When we evoke our senses this way, we are evoking our imaginations. But the more detail we give, the less our imaginations need to work (to fill in the blanks), and there's a cut-off point between supplying too much information and making a sale.

As you work through this book, you'll discover how to put these concepts into use and produce world beating copy. But before we continue with that, there's one more thing you need to know about getting attention.

What's love got to do with it?

Tied up with our synapses, senses, and desire to take action is emotion. Emotion comes from the Latin emovere, which means out-move. Since that is somewhat unhelpful and ambiguous, the French changed its meaning to what we now call emotions.

But before we explore that (and it matters very much that we do), here's what Wikipedia has to say about emotion: "There is currently no scientific consensus on a definition."

The etymology of emovere also comes from the Latin, which in this case, is the verb movere (to move). So we now know emotion is all about movement. Movement is action, which means if we want people to take action on our offers, emotion is going to play an important (and perhaps the most important) part.

The more I can move prospective customers (also known as prospects) to take action, the more action is likely to happen, so the more I play around with invoking emotional responses, the more likely my copy is to convert.

3 Hope and fear

Without hope we have nothing. The world survives only on hope. Of all our emotions, this is the one that keeps us alive (you may have thought it was FEAR, but fear drives us backwards ultimately to destruction, whereas hope ALWAYS drives us forwards).

A piece of copy without hope embedded in it somewhere will almost always fail. The only exception is fear using coercion (e.g., a government tax demand - "pay up or suffer the consequences" - but even with this there is hope - the hope that if we do what is asked, the fear will go away).

What is hope?

Google's definition: "a feeling of expectation and desire for a particular thing to happen." Hope, like all emotions, is a chemical reaction in our bodies.

Our job as copywriters is to know about those chemicals and discover the right words to use in the right order to invoke them.

DOSE

Here are the most common chemicals. They are easy to remember using the DOSE acronym:
1. Dopamine
2. Oxytocin
3. Serotonin
4. Endorphins

Dopamine

Dopamine is a neurotransmitter that sends signals triggered when we're expecting something good to happen. If our copy hints at being able to deliver something the reader desires, it will trigger an influx of dopamine.

When done well, at that point in a piece of copy, the reader is EXPECTING to find out more because their brains have been primed for exactly that. It's part of the influence process all copywriters rely on to deliver a return on investment for the cost of getting a message in front of the intended audience.

Dopamine is your new best friend and should now be swimming around your head as you read this. If you want people to feel they're about to be rewarded for reading your copy, turn on the dopamine trigger (you'll see how this comes together as we continue the journey through the rest of this book).

Oxytocin

Oxytocin is somewhat of a double-edged sword according to research by Northwestern University, Illinois (it can increase fear as you'll see in a second), that aside, oxytocin is known as the love drug.

If we need to elicit a certain amount of bonding between ourselves and our audience, oxytocin is our hormone of choice.

Like all these chemicals, we're not manufacturing and delivering them to our readers, we're writing the words that will help readers generate it for themselves.

And like everything in life, if there's the slightest whiff of doubt, the chemicals quickly turn bad. Oxytocin is no exception and can induce bad memories (and therefore feelings) about whomever has attempted to use subversion (the double-edged sword).

Serotonin

Serotonin is called the happy hormone. When we feel happy, it's because we have serotonin roaming around. If you want your readers to feel happy, send some sweet messages about how great it is to be happy, and voila, a dose of serotonin will follow.

Serotonin can also be introduced by physical activity. It's why people who suffer from depression or other serious mental conditions find that exercise can help (dopamine is good for this as well). It's also why a walk out in the sunshine makes us smile because vitamin D, which comes from the sun, is known to increase serotonin levels.

If you were writing a sequence of self-help emails as part of a larger campaign to sell exercise equipment or supplements, showing happy people taking exercise will help more than you may realise (now you know more about why happy images can work better than unhappy ones).

Endorphins

Endorphins calm us down. They have an opiate like effect. Anything that makes us feel good about ourselves (thus reducing stress) releases endorphins.

Be careful with this one though. If you remove all the tension and stress, your prospect may not want to do anything at all.

Cocktail

The best way to use DOSE is by combining the elements you believe will generate the best emotions you need to build desire and make a sale.

That can be done one hormone at a time. Perhaps some dopamine at the start (e.g., suggest some type of reward that will excite the reader: "keep reading to discover the secret of xyz"), then a little serotonin (e.g., "and imagine how that will make you feel when you finally get the results you were expecting"), plus a little oxytocin (e.g., "and it's not just you who'll feel the benefits here, your loved ones will too") and perhaps a sprinkling of endorphins (e.g., "with our step by step guide included, you'll never need to worry again").

How to use hope

You've just seen some examples of how to use hope using the DOSE framework. But that's only one of many.

Another is by using future-scaping.

This is also the main method used by highly paid consultants to close deals. Every one of us is in one of three states of mind at any given time. Either we're thinking about the past, the present (now), or the future.

Since hope resides ONLY in the future, it makes sense to think about what that future could look like if we were allowed to create it in any way we wanted. The same applies to our prospects.

Showing them the difference between what their lives look like now and what they might look like if they were to make certain changes (e.g., buying our product) is at the heart of future-scaping.

If we can convince any prospect that we understand how they're feeling now and we know how to make that feeling better, then we have a very good chance of getting their attention.

For example, here's a snippet of a piece of copy that encapsulates the journey we want a prospect to take if they're frustrated with their life and are seeking a new way to live:

"Having a 9 to 5 job is one way to earn a living, but it's not the only way. Suppose you could choose the hours you wanted to work, and not only that, choose the actual days you wanted to work as well."

We just future-scaped them from the current moment to a possible new (and better) future. That's all there is to it. Compare the present with the future and make the future look better.

You can see why this works so well for anyone wondering how to pitch a product or service in the consulting world - who doesn't want a glimpse of the future they yearn for?

Putting everything above together, it becomes clear that HOPE is the key to successful copy (there's no hope without a future, and no future without hope).

Fear

Coming back to fear again, I've written a whole appendix dedicated to it. Fear plays second fiddle to hope (as you may have already realised), but it still has its place in copy - just so long as it's not used for villainous purposes - which it frequently is - see Appendix F - Fear.

On the other hand, if you're a villain, good luck to you and I hope that eventually you'll realise you can get everything you need using hope and truth.

4 Change

Whilst copywriting and hope are inseparable, and there is no future without hope, another insight becomes clear: to get from the present moment to the future, something needs to change. This applies just as much to us as it does to our future prospects.

This is assuming of course, that we've been trying to get to that future without success (otherwise we'd be there and we'd no longer be reading this, or perhaps, any other book on copywriting).

There's something else you need to take on board as you've been reading along. Every aspect of copywriting doesn't just apply to you or your prospects, it matters to your prospects' customers too. Our goal is for everyone to be successful.

In other words, everything you learn here is universal. It will help you achieve your dream, your clients achieve their dream, and your clients' customers get what they want.

I need to make this clearer so let's go a little deeper. Every business to business or business to consumer transaction involves a number of players. All their problems are connected, that is, every person involved in the transaction, from you (writing copy), to your clients wanting to sell more, to their customers needing what they're selling, are suffering from the same basic problems - all of them **need** or **want** something.

The ONLY way for that to happen involves that same magic word: CHANGE (without change, nothing happens).

This means we have to identify the changes required for everyone to get what they want. For you, it might be a new client or more work from an existing client. For your client it might be to get more customers, or get more money from existing customers, or both.

For their customers it's always the same thing though. To fix a problem. Right now they have a problem, and it's a problem they hope will be fixed as fast as possible.

This represents both a pattern and a premise. The premise is that we exist to fix problems and everyone who shows an interest in us has that problem.

The pattern is that our market consists of 3 players (you, your client, your client's customers), and those 3 players are always in a state of change that we can influence (for as long as they and us remain players).

How to change

Let's start with you. You are where you are because of everything you've done in the past (and are doing right now). There are other influences affecting this of course, but since they're all external, we have very little control over them.

NOTE: Never be taken in by the common misconception that money buys success. It doesn't. The vast majority of advertising campaigns fail no matter how much money is poured into them - the only thing that money does in these cases is prove that the campaign failed.

This means we need to identify everything we're doing now that's keeping us where we are (what we've done in the past is irrelevant other than knowing it didn't particularly help and we need to avoid doing it again).

What's the first thing you need to change?

Start by making a list of everything you do during the day from the time you get up to the time you go to sleep. Don't miss anything out. Do this for a week. This is your FIRST change.

It's not a change you'll be doing every week, just a change from your normal routine to help you see the difference ANY change makes to your life.

This matters more than you may realise, but the difference it makes represents the start of a NEW you (an awesome copywriter) as well as a NEW future.

To learn anything new means change, which is why the focus in this chapter is on doing that. You CANNOT be the old you and become a professional copywriter without first making the necessary changes. It's impossible to succeed without it.

NOTE: The real first step you made was deciding you wanted to be a copywriter. That is fine, but it may be a repeating pattern that failed every time you decided to do something different but never followed through - e.g., you bought a book, took a course, went to a seminar, but didn't finish, follow up, or implement what you learnt.

What happens when I change?

I acted as a volunteer mentor for many years, and one thing that stood out in every case (and I do mean every case) was the friction and opposition my mentees got from those close to them - especially families and friends.

The reason is fear. Those close to them have only ever known the person who is about to make a lifestyle change as the person they once were, so the fear is that that person will become someone they (and others) no longer recognise.

This is understandable. If you married someone because of the way they are, then how are you going to feel if they decide to become someone completely different?

There is only one way to combat this, which I call the compassion weapon. Until you realise why they're raining on your parade, you'll never be able to reassure them why these changes are necessary. But once you do (because they are fearful of change) you bring out your compassion weapon by letting them know that whilst you'll be doing things differently from now on, underneath it will always be you, albeit with a new purpose, mission, and vision (PMV - more on that shortly).

What else do I need to change?

Grab your list of current daily activities and put a tick against each one that you know for certain is helping you become a copywriter. For example, "writing copy", "reading."

Then put a cross against each item that is NOT helping you become a copywriter

NOTE: Activities like "family time", "holiday", "eating dinner", "sleeping", "cleaning teeth" will ALWAYS have a tick, since your health (mental and physical) will always be more important than any career.

If you didn't have 'writing and reading' on your list, add them now. They're your top priority. Great copywriters read everything they can including fiction, non-fiction and every ad they ever come across.

You need to have these habitualised so they become something you not only do automatically, but look forward to doing with enthusiasm. The easiest way to create any new habit is to associate it with something you have already habitualised.

For example, if you always have breakfast, you can associate writing with it by getting into the habit of going into your office directly afterwards and getting stuck straight into your first writing task of the day. Since breakfast is something most people enjoy, you will be adding further joy by knowing that breakfast is your trigger to get creative.

You may want to leave a post-it note on the table the night before to remind you of the new habit you're about to create. You could also associate that post-it note with doing your teeth before you go to bed by leaving it stuck to the bathroom mirror so you never forget.

If you don't do something like this to help you get in the habit of writing every day, nothing will change. But if you do, wonderful things will happen.

Do the same for reading too. For me, that's something I do just before I go to sleep and after I've written my daily journal (another writing habit I developed that has paid dividends).

What if I fail to make the change stick?

The trouble with habits is we give up too early. New Year resolutions are of course the best example. We're fired up to make the change only to get bored before it takes hold. That happens for one reason. We try to do too much in too short a time. We raise our expectations (or have them raised for us by great copywriters selling us ideas about how to change our lives) and when nothing happens in a week, we give up on it and return to our former (highly habitualised with the wrong habits) way of life.

The way out of that is to remember two things:

1. Never overdo it. To develop a writing habit, start by writing ONE sentence a day.
2. Do it at your prescribed (and soon to be habitualised) writing time.

Every habit we ever created took time to become a habit. For me, it took well over a year before I became a habitual daily journal writer. Now it's become my best friend. If I don't write my daily journal as soon as I jump into bed, I start missing it. It's where I can write my innermost thoughts without fear or consequence.

If you've followed any of the many self-help gurus out there, you'll know most of them recommend reading a book a week (and many claim they read a book a day).

I've taken speed reading courses with the promise I can get through even more books, but whenever I resort to that method, I find I miss the enjoyment of speaking each word to myself (which is why we read slowly), so I read at the same speed I've always done - slowly and with care.

It doesn't matter how many books you read (or even how fast you read them provided you take in their message) it just matters that you do it, and you do it every day (even if you pick up a book and read ONE sentence). Change ONLY happens when you habitualise it.

Are there any other habits I need to develop?

Perfectionism. Everyone tells you perfectionism is bad. They're wrong. They mistake perfectionism for procrastination. If your writing is not as perfect as YOU can make it in the TIME given, then it won't be good enough for your clients either (because you won't have the confidence to sell it to them).

There is this notion that good enough is good enough, but this is only true when we don't particularly care about our output. Don't fall into that trap. The more time you take to care about what you do for your clients, the more they will care about you.

Perfection means doing something to the best of your ability at that point in time. When we go wrong, it's because of our vanity. We have this deep belief that everyone is watching for every word we say or deed we do. When the reality is most people only care about themselves.

It's not surprising we have this attitude. For most of us, we were brought up that way. The more we were scolded, the more fearful we became, until as adults, we daren't break

35

the status quo. It's why change is so hard (we often care more about what other people think about us than what we think about ourselves).

But know this. Whatever you write today will not live up to your future self's critique of it. In other words, the more you write, the better you get. This is another reason people tell us that good enough is good enough, but the good enough we're after is the perfection we can achieve today (not the perfection of tomorrow).

Precious

This is perhaps the most important lesson to learn from this chapter on Change. Never be precious about your writing. If you think you just wrote the most important thing ever written in the history of writing, KNOW that tomorrow you will write something better (and that you'll most likely look back to today with disgust).

Get used to throwing away words, sentences, and paragraphs. The more you do it, the less precious you will be, and the less stress you will get. KNOW that not only will you write something better tomorrow, but it will ALWAYS be that way.

I learned this lesson when I wrote the book, Accounting for Everyone in the mid 1990's. Half way through I lost the lot. I'd written it on an Acorn Archimedes computer and hadn't backed up a thing.

I was gutted. But a week later, I got my mojo back and started again, only this time, I already knew what I wanted to say (I'd spent over a year thinking and writing about it).

Most of the words were already in my mind, so it was just a matter of spilling them back onto the page.

However, this time they were better. I made copious backups from that point onwards but never needed a single one. When I finally completed and published the book in 1998 I knew it was a better book than the original version I'd lost.

I'll go into detail about editing later. It's MORE important than any ideas you dream up along the way (although it has to be said that no piece of copy will ever work as well as one supported by a big idea - more on that later too).

A final word on perfection

There's a story about a master potter. She had an apprentice, and asked that apprentice to make the best cup he could and bring it to her when completed. The apprentice followed the order and an hour later presented his newly minted cup.

The master potter looked at it, crushed it, and gave it back to him saying "not good enough, try again." This went on for the rest of the day. Every time, the cup got a little better.

At clocking off time the apprentice presented his final cup to the master potter. The master potter ignored the final cup, looked at the apprentice and asked "are you satisfied with this?"

The apprentice said "yes" and the cup was accepted. The difference between the final cup and all the others was the deadline. That's the only thing that matters. If we don't set a deadline, we will never finish anything.

A deadline defines perfect and always will do if we want change to happen. Make deadlines, stick to them, and you will find perfection in everything you do.

No going back

There are two things to know about change. First, nothing changes without it. Second, once you make that change and see the benefit, there's no going back (because you wouldn't want to).

The best changes become new habits, and once set, like all habits become hard to break (which is why making any change is hard and takes time).

The changes suggested at the start of this chapter are the start of a new you, and the rest of this book will help you get the most from it.

5 Purpose, mission, and vision (PMV)

Remember your PMV at all times. What is your PMV? Read on.

Mission

A mission is something you feel you have to do. What's yours? Write it down in a single sentence. If it's longer than a single sentence, you'll never complete it (and it's almost certain you're over-complicating it). And, if after editing, it still feels too long, you're probably trying to mix multiple missions into the single mission you'll need to adopt if you want to make the changes you need to make to become a professional copywriter.

NOTE: in the previous paragraph I've used a couple of rhetorical devices. We'll go into that later - and also in Appendix D - Rhetoric, but if something you read gets your attention, there's every chance a rhetorical device has been used.

How to get clear on your mission

To get clarity on your mission, start with your vision. What sort of world do you want to live in? Can you clearly visualise it? This is the world you will be creating. View it as though it were complete, so you can SEE the world the way you want it to be and you'll have a vision worth fighting for.

Heroes and villains

For me it's **a world full of heroic copywriters writing for heroic businesses**. That's my vision. Imagine a world where the only copywriters that count are those fighting for the force of good, and the only businesses that survive are those who truly care about their customers, their products, and the world.

It doesn't matter if that's a pipedream, a utopian impossibility, or an ideal world that will never happen, it's still the world I want to see, and I will do all I can to make it so.

Villains

We live in a world of heroes and villains. The villains are there to tear us down, to lie, cheat, and steal their way to the top (doing whatever it takes to get what they want).

The villains' mission is to destroy the world (although they don't see it that way). The heroes' mission is to save it from destruction.

Villains love and uphold violence in the pretence that it's a force for good (they use rhetorical terms like 'law and order' to promote themselves and gain control of the people). They are the fascists of the world. A world run by villains is uncomfortable for everyone, including, the villains (who must surround themselves with protection at all times).

Heroes

True heroes don't care about protection. They know it's not about themselves but the world as a whole - and they understand they are here to play their part in it.

True heroes care about people - all the people. They know that villains exist for two reasons, first, because they are fearful of the world, and second, because they know no better. True heroes have compassion, even for the villains.

The fundamental difference between heroes and villains is they care not just for people, but for the whole planet (animal, vegetable, and mineral). If you adopt a similar philosophy, you'll find it a LOT easier to produce better copy.

Empathy

Copy that converts is copy that understands its audience. Copy that has no idea about its audience won't convert. Writing empathetic copy is one solution.

If I know what makes you tick and why you do the things you do, then I can write copy that presses those buttons and gets you to do what I want you to do, which is this: buy whatever it is that is going to fix your current most pressing problem.

If you don't have a current pressing problem, then no matter what I do, my copy will fail to sell you anything other than a new opinion on something. But that matters too. It's part of the buyer's journey, and a hugely important part of educating a market and scaling a business.

Creating a need where one currently doesn't exist is impossible, but creating a want is a different thing altogether.

Needs and wants

Make your purpose, mission, and vision, needs based (not wants based). A need needs to be satisfied. A want does not. I may want a world of hero copywriters and businesses, but I also know the world NEEDS this if we're to have any chance of avoiding the path to destruction.

We MUST care about our planet as it's the only thing we've got. Let's use a little bit of rhetoric to ram this home (if you're unsure about this whole hero versus villain business, then I need to ensure you become certain of its importance, or I fail).

The Science of Rhetoric is 2000+ years old. The Greeks coined the term and came up with hundreds of rules that the great orators of this world know about. If you want to learn persuasion, the rules of rhetoric have just become your new best friends.

Each rule has a name, and one of those is called Reductio ad Absurdum. It means 'take it to the limit' (or, reduce to the absurd).

If it takes mining our planet for enough resources to get us to the next planet in order to escape our solar system's inevitable destruction by its own sun then we're going to have to do the same to the next planet too, and so on, until there are no planets or solar systems left to escape to. In other words, mining our planet is a BAD thing - it's not progress.

We may WANT to 'have it all', but we don't NEED to have it all. For a vision to make any sense then, we need to look for the NEEDS of those we want to influence (our audience).

As copywriters, our audience consists of businesses or organisations (profit and non-profit). We can choose to target them all in the hope that some will bite, but if we do, we will either become a commodity copywriter (meaning we may not get paid what we need) or we won't be heard at all (because the market, like all markets, is saturated with commodities).

So we choose a specific type of audience who all have ONE thing in common - a need for our services. They're often to be found in what's called a vertical market, which might be a specific type of business (e.g., a dentist) or a demographic such as the FTSE 100 register of businesses in the UK or the Fortune 500 register of businesses in the USA.

From there we can niche down further if we're still not sure what our audience needs. For example, do they need more sales? Do they need more customers? Do they need better products (or someone to position their products in a better light)?

Do they need stronger branding (and someone to write better copy that shows clearly how superior they are)?

Do they need a champion to prove to the world they care more about their customers than anyone else in their industry? (that might look more like the sort of thing a public relations professional may do, but it's still copy in the context of persuasion).

Whatever the needs are of the audience you choose to target, your mission is to fulfil those needs.

Just make sure that once you've fulfilled every person in your market's top need, the world you've created from it matches your vision.

Purpose

Your purpose is your why. Your mission is how you will fulfil your purpose. But underneath all of it is philosophy.

Philosophy is not just my favourite subject, but the world's too. More has been written on it than any other topic. Philosophy is how we each see the world.

Philosophy is a mixture of knowledge and belief. This is why it's different for everyone. We each have a philosophy (a belief or first-hand knowledge) of every individual part of everything in our world.

If I talk about money, you'll have an opinion on it. Whatever that opinion is, it becomes your philosophy on it, and will REFLECT everything you think and do about it. For example, if you believe money (or even the love of money) is the root of all evil, then it will become the root of all evil and you will do your best to avoid it, but if you're a villain, you'll probably lie, cheat, and steal your way to get as much of it as you can.

If your purpose is to become a hero copywriter for not-for-profit organisations fighting for change in the world, then your mission will be to help those organisations achieve it.

If your mission is to become the highest paid copywriter on the planet, then you may be lacking in empathy for your audience (the ones who will make you rich) so think carefully about your purpose and why that purpose matters, not to you, but to your clients.

Note that how much you earn from copywriting is directly proportional to the value you give to your clients. The more value you give, the more you can earn.

Vision

By now you'll have a clear understanding of why vision matters. If you cannot see what the end result of your mission looks like, you'll have no idea if you've achieved it, but more importantly, you'll have no chance of getting there anyway.

As you work through this book, it is likely your vision will change. That's fine. Most people don't have a vision and never will. That's why most of us sleepwalk through life. If we can't see the future, then there is no future to see.

The most successful people on this planet clearly see their future. They know what their mission is, and above all they know why they're committed to achieving it. To join them, start by dreaming about the world you want to see and live in.

Copywriting is used in every walk of human life. No matter how big or ambitious your dream, it's going to need words, carefully thought about and written words, to make it real.

Here's the journey of all human endeavour:

Thought > Words > Action > Result

In the next chapter we'll go deeper and begin the process of figuring out your PMV.

6 Niches

Every piece of copy solves a problem. Remember this at all times. Especially when you've just finished a piece and are checking it over. Ask yourself what problem did this copy solve? If you have no clear answer, you'll need to rewrite it because it will have failed to do its job.

Some content pieces also solve a problem, but that doesn't make it copy as in sales copy, which is what this book is about (in other words, if you're writing some informative content - as opposed to sales copy, this rule only applies if that content is meant to solve a problem).

Every problem (including the problems we have, our clients have, and our clients' customers have) is based on a need or a want.

The difference between a need and a want is this: Needs MUST be solved. Wants can be left dangling forever.

Industries

Every niche has a series of problems that need solving. The more problems there are to be solved, the bigger the niche. That size may depend on the number of people in the niche, or the number of problems each person in the niche has.

For example, everyone involved in the food industry has the same need: to supply or consume food. It is the most NEEDY industry on the planet (the next most needy industry is health, and the next after that is security followed by wealth and leisure).

1. Food
2. Health
3. Security
4. Wealth
5. Leisure

You could argue that leisure is not a need at all, but think of the worker slaving away all year and their need to take a break every now and then. That's when the idea of a holiday becomes a need.

Wealth is also borderline until you realise that no wealth at all means you can't buy your number one need - food (let alone health or security).

There are more startups in the food industry than any other, and once you know the hierarchy of needful things: Food > Health > Security > Wealth > Leisure, it's obvious why.

You might be wondering where the more esoteric industries fit in, such as fashion. Fashion is clothing, and clothing is security, so it slots in along with other industries like housing (e.g., the real estate industry).

You can also see that whilst luxury brands fit into every needful sector, they are distinguished by being a WANT (we may NEED a car, but some of us would prefer a luxury car, which is more of a WANT).

Commodities

This takes us into the difference between needs and wants within industries. Every WANT slots into the same list of needs. So are they as important as needs? Is there also a hierarchy of wants? Yes and no.

Whilst there is a hierarchy of wants, it cannot be evaluated in the same way.

The need for commodities is consistent. We must have food to survive. We must have health to operate in any meaningful way. And it's only when we can eat and are healthy that security enters the frame.

Once those three needs are in place, we can think about wealth, and from there, we can find ourselves able to afford luxuries.

Status

Compare the needs market to the wants market. Wants are driven by an entirely different set of criteria.

For example, status is perhaps the top driver of luxuries. Why eat beans on toast when you can have Russian caviar served up in the most prestigious Michelin 3-star restaurant on the planet? (I'd actually prefer fresh fruit, but that's because I made a choice to eat more healthily, which makes me the wrong audience to sell luxury food to - a reminder about the importance of knowing who you're selling to).

Comfort

Another driver of the wants market is comfort. I'd rather stay at a 5-star hotel than in a tent (whereas when I was younger, the tent was by far my top preference - wants change over time).

Status and comfort are two attributes of the luxury market. Once you're aware of these attributes, it becomes much easier to write compelling copy. When you know what drives your market, you can get inside their heads and help them make the right decision (because that's what heroic copywriting means - helping our clients and customers make the right choices for them).

Niches within niches

As a newly fledged copywriter, you don't have to choose an industry, and indeed most don't. But as a professional (and well paid) copywriter, you would do well to consider it right from the start.

This is the old 'generalist versus specialist' argument. We'd all choose a specialist over a generalist if our need was great. If we chose to write for the health industry, and within that decided on becoming the go to person for medical doctors and consultants, we'd beat ALL other copywriters who did not champion these people in their sales messages.

In other words, if I were a consulting surgeon looking to hire a copywriter to help launch a new book I'd written, I'd want someone who knew my profession inside out. It would also help me make up my mind if they knew how to write copy to launch books as well.

This example highlights an interesting aspect of how to position yourself in a market. Within any niche, there are any number of problems. Each of those problems is its own niche, but if we were just to pick one of those niches within niches (e.g., a medical copywriter specialising in launching books), our market would almost certainly be too narrow (e.g., how many consulting surgeons are there in the world right now who are just about to launch a book?).

Taking this further, consultant surgeons don't often write books (although if you were able to solve that, you would become their first choice assuming there was no one else claiming the same thing).

So I suggest considering a niche that's small enough to stand out, yet large enough to support your business, a goal. It doesn't have to be your first goal, but keep it in mind in your early years (if you're not sure what to choose, your early clients will choose it for you, but it may not turn out to be what you want). More on that in a second.

Another example of a niche within a niche is a specialist biography copywriter. In the medical world, every consultant who speaks publicly, has a website, or who has a prominent position, will also need a professional set of biographical notes written about them (e.g., for use on an 'About us' page on a website - often referred to as a 'bio').

That need is driven by those seeking to find out more about that particular person. A good bio sells a person to the audience that person wants to attract. So it's closer to sales copy than it is to content (a great copywriter will write in a way that's non-salesy too).

Whilst a task like that may be handled by, in the case of a convention or seminar, the event's organisers or marketing team, they too will need to find someone who can write copy designed to sell each individual speaker to the prospective audience (it's often an in-house role, but there are plenty of freelance event organisers around, and getting on their books as their goto copy person is a great way to start a copywriting career).

This may seem like an odd example, but someone has to do it, and, since those in a position of status don't want to be associated with bad copy (as it's not good for their reputation), they will always prefer to hire someone who won't let them down and who will also show them in the best light. And for that, they will pay a premium.

The more you dig into an industry, the more opportunities you will uncover within each industry to find and exploit.

How to choose an industry

We know that the number one industry in the world is food, so if you're looking for the easiest ride of all, that's a great place to start. However, as it's more commodity driven than any other industry (because above all else, we all need food to survive) it means there's more competition.

Don't let that hold you back though. Every industry is full of competition. It goes with the territory. If we as humans have earmarked something that matters, it's because there is a demand for it (demand = problem to be solved).

And where there's demand, there will always be someone ready and willing to step up and provide a solution.

So now the question becomes: how do I stand out from the crowd?

Before we get into that, try choosing one of the major NEEDS industries from the list (Food, Health, Security, Wealth, Leisure) and start researching which section within that industry you'd feel most at home with. For example in food, that might be a choice of vegan, organic, healthy, ready meals, restaurants, manufacturers, distributors etc.

Whatever you choose, make it something you already know something about or are interested in exploring. This will help keep you motivated. Remember one thing though, until you're confident in your writing ability, you'll never be able to sell yourself no matter what niche you choose. So that's where we're headed next - how to write commanding copy.

7 How to write commanding copy

What's your top value? Given a choice of only one thing in life, what would you choose?

This is a tough question because the choice seems infinite. It's an 'open question'. The responder needs to use their brain to come up with an answer, and the first answer that springs to mind is rarely the answer they will finally settle upon.

We also don't know what that one 'thing' may be because we don't know the context - we haven't been told the big picture or why we're even being asked this question, so we fill in the missing pieces as best we can.

Bad copy works like that. It tries to lead but fails. People are left confused. They can't make a decision because they don't know what it is they need to decide.

If I offer you 3 price points without letting you know what you get, you will choose none and walk away.

The clue here is the word LEAD. In copywriting (and journalism), this is also called LEDE or LEADER. It's the opening few paragraphs (it might even just be the first sentence).

Its purpose is to hook the reader into wanting to read more. The headline acts in the same way. As is well known in copywriting circles, the purpose of the headline is to get people to read the first sentence. The purpose of the first sentence is to get people to read the second sentence, and so on (see the RULES section).

To make a lead work, you will need a BIG IDEA. David Ogilvy coined the phrase "big idea" in the 1960's:

"It takes a big idea to attract the attention of consumers and get them to buy your product. Unless your advertising contains a big idea, it will pass like a ship in the night. I doubt if more than one campaign in a hundred contains a big idea."

Note that last sentence. It sums up advertising and tells us there is always an edge to be found. Scan a bunch of ads today (both online and in print) and you'll see nothing much has changed.

So what is a big idea? It's something new. It doesn't have to be a new 'new', just different. In fact, one of the biggest ideas in advertising is the word NEW itself. It sells because it gets to the heart of consumerism - the DESIRE for something NEW is somehow very attractive to human beings (if you're ever stuck for a new idea, just use the word NEW).

People often talk of hooks and angles in copy. They're simply implementations of big ideas (see Rule 8). Where a big idea is something new or different (often from a metaphysical point of view - e.g., "the sun never sets because it's always rising somewhere in the world"), a hook or angle represents the conversion of that big idea into something concrete that connects perfectly with what we're selling (e.g., "The Perpetual Pen runs on practically forever just like the sun").

The 2020 UK Coca-Cola campaign uses this slogan as a Big Idea: "Open Like Never Before." I had no idea what that meant when I first read it, nor would anyone else unless they had time to find out more.

They're using intrigue and innuendo to get us to find out more. Did it work? I've no idea, it's the sort of data Coca-Cola would only make public if it sold a billion (or won an award).

My first thought was "open more Coke bottles?" Perhaps that's the hidden message. We all know what Coke is. We know it's for sale, and we know the Coca-Cola company's job is to sell as much cola as they can.

Clicking through from that slogan on the Coca-Cola UK site, they tell me it means Be More Open (so I completely misunderstood it). They're trying to tap into the zeitgeist of our ever more authoritarian world and how we can somehow get back the ONE value we all REALLY strive for - Freedom (or maybe it was because so many things were closed due to COVID-19 except Coke - who knows, but one thing is certain, this Big Idea probably failed - I never saw that campaign ad again).

There was also a connection with the UK government's messaging of "opening up the UK" after the lockdown. So it looks like the big idea was more about getting some extra publicity off the government's own PR campaign.

Or perhaps the researchers figured that the British public believed more in opening up the country to business again than in staying at home. Only time will tell, but the point is, maybe the big idea of the campaign was 'Back to Work' - a kind of freedom for many (having been stuck at home for months).

If I were advising Coca-Cola, this campaign wouldn't have seen the light of day. Why? Because of the confusion it causes. David Ogilvy would be laughing his head off or turning in his grave were he to have seen it.

Values

We only buy things we value. Remember that. If we don't value something, it means it is worth ZERO to us. We couldn't even give it away (many have tried and failed).

The current trend for an eBook in return for an email address is fine provided the eBook has value to the prospective subscriber, but how do we know when no money is being exchanged?

The true answer is we don't. Many people purchase things they never use (especially digital products), but this gives us an idea of how we might test such an offer.

Suppose we're writing for a client who runs a book shop specialising in sailing and who has tasked us with lead generation to build a mailing list of sailing fans. We've been hired to not just write the words, but to come up with a complete lead generation campaign.

How would we start? Well, it's always the same no matter what niche or industry we're in. We start with the audience, and the first question we need to ask is what is it they value?

If you ask random people the same question, you'll get back a blank stare, so we need to make it easier. To do that, we research the market and make a list of all the products in that market (sailing books in our example).

Then we sort the list into the most popular (i.e., most valued) and then sort again by most expensive (so we have some idea of the profit margin).

Think of these lists as 'features' (we haven't gone into why these features are useful yet - we'll do that later when we look into the benefits). Here are some sample lists so you can see what I'm getting at (I used Amazon as my research tool):

Best-selling sailing books

To get this list, I searched for Sailing Books directly in Amazon, then sorted them by 'average customer review' (these lists vary every day and are likely to be different in every country - however, they do give you a bird's eye view into what's selling right now):

1. For The Love Of The Sea (Novel)
2. How To Read Water
3. The One That Got Away (Novel)
4. Day Skipper Handbook
5. The Complete Sailing Manual
6. The Summer Isles (Travel book)
7. Knot Know-How
8. An Introduction to Navigation
9. A Seaman's Guide to the Rule of the Road
10. The Klutz Book of Knots

7 of the 10 books are nonfiction practical guides. 1 is a travel book. And 2 are novels with a sea connection.

Highest value best-selling sailing books

Now I sort the same set of books by price (highest first) - this has to be done outside of Amazon or you'll get a completely different set of books.

1. The Complete Sailing Manual
2. Day Skipper Handbook
3. A Seaman's Guide to the Rule of the Road
4. An Introduction to Navigation
5. How To Read Water
6. The Summer Isles
7. The Klutz Book of Knots
8. Knot Know-How
9. The One That Got Away (Novel)
10. For The Love Of The Sea (Novel)

The two novels move from the top to the bottom of the list when it comes to cost. They were priced £1.99 and £2.99 respectively. We don't know if they became best sellers because they were bought by our target audience or because of their authors' popularity or simply the low price, but what we do know is the most valued books are non-fiction, and the highest priced book of all has a title that implies it gives our audience everything they could ever want: "The Complete Sailing Manual."

It's also number 5 in our best-selling list, so it's right up there in terms of audience interest (if you factor out the 2 novels, it's the third most popular book).

The second most popular book is the Day Skipper Handbook, and that also proves to be the second most valuable book.

So with hardly any research at all, we now have a very good idea of what our audience craves. They want to know all about how to sail, and they want to know how to sail as a skipper or captain of a boat.

The next step is to figure out a lead magnet that our audience would value almost as much as owning those books.

NOTE: A lead magnet is something we can give away in return for contact details - usually an email address so we can contact them again and hopefully sell them something.

The lead magnet may be some kind of checklist. It could be a report or summary of the books. It might be an explainer video, or any number of other options.

But rather than creating a single lead magnet (by, say, combining a summary of the top books into one) we could create separate lead magnets for each of them and not only test them against each other, we can use them to generate multiple lead streams (this is part of a segmentation process we'll get to later).

How to create a lead magnet

Lead magnets need to be short. But they must still be valuable, and one way to do this is by looking at the chapter titles shown in the table of contents pages of the top books.

We're not plagiarising these books. We're using them as research tools. This is easy with books since you can compile lists of the table of contents pages of all the top books in any niche and you should come up with a list of everything relevant to that niche (Amazon's "Look Inside..." feature makes this easy).

Armed with that, coming up with a title and compiling, say, a Sailing Checklist as a lead magnet is simple.

For example, the second item in The Complete Sailing Manual's table of contents page is called 'Parts of a boat'. Using that (together with research from other online sources) would make creating, say, an infographic showing a sailing boat and all its parts simple.

You might even go on to create more than one infographic highlighting different boats. You can find thousands of free images online to spice it up, or use any of the free or paid graphic creation programs out there.

How to market a lead magnet

Lead magnets, like anything else, need the right words to sell them (free is rarely free - it takes time to read an eBook or report - time we're asking our prospects to give us along with their email address - that's a BIG ask).

But before we can think about the words we're going to use, we need to be clear about the purpose of the lead magnet - and not just the obvious purpose - to build or grow a list, but what we're going to do with that list - and that requires something called systems thinking.

Systems thinking

A system is something whole. It has a purpose. All systems work in conjunction with the parts that make the system up as well as everything surrounded by the system or connected with it.

Each human life is an example of a system. We have a fairly good idea of the length of an average human life, we know its purpose (to create and/or nurture), and we know roughly how the system works (we're born, we learn, we do things, and we die - I realise that sounds rather blunt, but we're talking systems here, and if we're to be honest about it, we cannot afford to ignore the truth).

NOTE: If you disagree with my notions of the life and purpose of humans, that's fine, insert some other objective in its place that you are more comfortable with, just remember that systems work because they're better than the alternative - chaos.

What is systems thinking? If we isolate and improve one part of a system without thinking about the system as a whole, we run a high risk of messing up the system. For example, if we decide the purpose of a lead magnet campaign is to get as many click-throughs as possible from an ad without knowing the quality of those clicks, we run the risk of creating a list of clickers and not the list of buyers we were really looking for.

In short, a system consists of many parts working in partnership. It's no good improving one part of the system without understanding how that improvement will help (or more importantly, affect) the other parts.

Lead magnet audience

In our example campaign, the owner of the bookshop wants a list to send out a catalogue of sailing books to. Therefore we want people who are not only interested in sailing, but like to read books about it too.

Since, in my experience, the world is divided into people who prefer to read books, and people who prefer to listen to audio, it's clear we only want to attract one particular type - a reader, rather than a listener.

Just as our prospects, customers, and clients are divided, it's the same with copywriters - some prefer books and reading, whilst others prefer video and audio. That's fine, since both involve words. However, those who prefer books and reading have an advantage. And that advantage is patience.

They are happier to spend as long as it takes to get their words just right, rather than good enough. Someone into audio books and video is more likely to be inclined to dictate copy than write it. Whilst that may be faster, editing takes a lot longer, and will require the time and expertise of someone external to the process.

Using systems thinking then, we need to know which type of audience we want to attract with our ads (readers or viewers).

Writing an ad

Once we know our audience, it helps us shape the ad we're going to write to sell the lead magnet. Here are the demographics of the people we want to attract for our example:

- Interested in sailing
- Like reading books
- Like collecting books

We don't care about their age, gender, social status, education, or political views at the moment (although we are likely to discover later that some or all of these have an effect).

We've narrowed down our market specifically, so an image for the ad is easy to envisage: some type of sailing vessel and perhaps an image of the sea will do nicely.

If we decide to create a boat parts infographic as a lead magnet, then the best image would probably be an exploded image of a boat - a kind of 'explainer' boat image if you like.

The purpose of an image in an ad

The purpose of any image in an ad is to attract attention. If the image is not aligned to the offer the ad is selling (in this case to build a list of people interested in sailing), then it will attract the wrong people (that of course is what click-bait is all about).

It's also often said that images that include smiling people work better than images that don't. To test that out (albeit rather unscientifically) I ran a series of 3 ads on Facebook.

They all promoted the same post - the one I used to announce to the world I was writing a diary to accompany the writing of this book from the day it was conceived to the day I finished it.

For the first ad, I used a standard (big smile) profile image of myself with an office in the background.

The second ad used an image generated by Facebook of the post I was promoting. It consisted of just words (not really an image at all in the usual sense).

And the third ad contained the ICA logo (just the abbreviation ICA with International Copywriters Association written underneath).

I ran them as separate campaigns targeting the same group of people (copywriters in the UK) so it was quite likely they would each see all 3 ads. My expectation was that the smiley face image would get the most clicks.

The results were the opposite. In third place with what proved to be the most expensive ad was the smiling face (less clicks, highest cost), second was the ICA logo, which meant the winning image was the one that consisted almost exclusively of words.

Targeting

It's very likely most aspiring copywriters find words interesting (and images of a smiling dude in an office uninteresting). Also, an image that simply says "ICA" with "International Copywriters Association" in small print underneath is perhaps less likely to be as interesting as something that contains a real message.

If that's true, then the results speak for themselves. For an audience of copywriters, a random image of someone smiling is less interesting than an image of a logo, and both those are less interesting than an image full of copywriting wisdom.

The cost of the winning ad was 36% cheaper than the worst ad. That's significant and is an example of what Facebook call Ad Relevance (this is called Quality Score on Google and has a similar effect - Google and Facebook want to reward advertisers by reducing their ad spend if it results in a better experience for their users because it keeps people coming back for more, and that means more advertising revenue overall).

What are the best words to use?

Up to this point, you'd be forgiven for thinking that copywriting is full of tricks of persuasion. After all, we're often led to believe that copywriting is something only a guru can teach and that only they know the secret of creating 6, 7, and 8 figure businesses.

They're wrong, the only trick at work in those cases is trickery itself. Yes, there are innocent people who will buy anything given a strong enough promise, but thankfully they only represent a small proportion of any given audience.

The majority are not so easily fooled, so it makes sense that the majority is the audience we are interested in - people who genuinely need what we are there to sell.

This will still be attractive to everyone interested of course, but that's fine when we write ethical copy there to sell quality products. The golden rule is to never over-promise.

So what exactly are the best words to use then?

66

Simple ones (see also rule 3 in chapter 12).

How simple? As simple as necessary. We want people to read our copy from beginning to end. We don't want them tripping up on words they don't understand, foreign words, or cliched phrases they've heard a thousand times before.

NOTE: Not all cliches are created equal, some cliches work fine in different contexts, but rules can only be broken when we know what they are and we know that they exist as a guide.

As kids, our imaginations are at their strongest. They've not been beaten back with age, so when we read a children's book as a child, we imagine far more than has been written (we only discover this when we reread those books as adults and wonder why it was we saw so much in them).

This happens because of the simple language used in those books. Children's book authors understand that the joy of reading comes not from using big words, but from the simplest possible.

The flow is what matters. When our writing flows like a stream without obstacles, it becomes a river that eventually turns into an ocean. The 13th century Persian poet Rumi said it like this: "You are not a drop in the ocean, but an ocean in a drop."

Rumi's quote is also an example of a Big Idea. When a piece of copy has a truly big idea at the heart of its message, that "ocean in a drop" turns into an ocean of attention.

The simplest words are usually the shortest ones. We could use 'forest' instead of 'wood' for example, but if we want people to see the wood for the trees, then wood is best. On the other hand, it's better to use forest if we're talking about a large wood. Think about every word.

Einstein had something to say on this: "Everything should be made as simple as possible, but no simpler." If I replaced the word 'simple' with 'easy' in his quote, it would lose its meaning.

Chapter 12 has the information you need to choose the right words (or rather, not choose the wrong words) and why these rules matter, but let's go into the practical side of this.

Why does some copy suck?

When we read anything, we come to it in a certain frame of mind. As copywriters, we have no idea what that frame of mind may be, but we do know there IS a frame of mind, and therefore we have some control over how to deal with it.

For example, if someone's looking for a solution to get more leads into their business, they may already have had their fingers burnt by people promising more than they can deliver (this is very common).

Knowing that, we can handle the objection up front. "Fed up with people promising to get you more leads, then badly letting you down?" With that one sentence, we've laid out our store and implied there's a strong offer coming.

But there's a problem with it. The problem is the adverb 'badly'. It sucks. Why? Because it's not necessary and takes away the gravity of the implied promise (which is: "we won't let you down - unlike the others").

Remove it and you get: "Fed up with people promising to get you more leads, then letting you down?"

In this example (and countless others), the adverb is a form of rhetoric called Hyperbole (see Appendix D). Hype is the shortened version of that word. We all know what hype is, but most of us have to look up the longer version before we realise that 'hype' is its abbreviation. If I were writing a textbook on rhetoric, I would use the word hyperbole, but if my audience were marketers I might use the word hype instead to help with the flow.

Right now, I'm following Einstein's advice on simple. I need to explain why copy sucks, and I need to do it in an authoritative way so I can help you write better copy.

I could have used the word "hype" from the outset, the trouble is, hype is not just an abbreviation, it's slang, and using slang is rarely a good idea. In fiction, characters can speak using slang (or colloquial words) but using slang in copy is risky unless you really know your audience.

So part of keeping things simple and unsucky is to remove all unnecessary adverbs (as well as foreign words, cliched phrases, and slang) and do it without removing the meaning.

Pronouns

Another big problem with amateur copy sounding sucky is the use of pronouns (see Chapter 12 Rule 6). If I use the pronoun 'I' all the time, it can sound boastful. If I use 'you' all the time, it can sound demanding. If I use nothing but 'him', 'her', and 'them' it can sound ranty.

The reason beginner copywriters struggle with pronouns is their lack of story (and by that, I mean understanding who a customer is, what they want, and where we want to take them).

Some of the most convincing stories use all three types of pronoun (i.e., first, second, and third person: I, you, they).

Copy can start in third person (using alignment to show that there are other people out there just like us, who also have the same problem we're trying to fix). Then move to first person to show the reader that the author was also just like them, and finally move to second person to let them know they can find a solution.

Copy can also start in first person (singular or plural - 'I' or 'We'), then move to third person for proof, and finally end up in second person for the close.

Going back to our example of the bookshop owner building their list for sailing books, here's how I might word a short ad that used an eBook about tying knots as a lead magnet:

"As kids we all remember the joy of tying knots. However, I struggled with many of them, so I searched online and came across The Simple Guide To Nautical Knots. As a result I no longer get my clove and cleat hitches mixed up. If you want to tie knots in your sleep, click here and download The Simple Guide To Nautical Knots today."

As a general rule, use first person to demonstrate that you suffered just like your reader did. In other words, use it to show empathy. Use third person as proof that others also suffered in the past ("they were not alone"). Use first and third person to show how you and others overcame that, and finally use second person to bring the reader into the story and show them they too can achieve success (just like you and others did).

This is just one example of how to use all three types of pronoun (first, second, and third person) to show how a future with your solution would benefit the reader.

But not all readers are the same, which brings us to awareness.

In the book Breakthrough Advertising (1966) Eugene Schwartz wrote about buyer awareness. The idea was that every prospect can be measured by one of five levels of awareness starting from completely unaware and leading to fully aware (or most aware as he called it).

Trying to sell anything to an unaware audience is the hardest thing to do not just because they're unaware of whatever is being sold, who the seller is, or whether there's even a problem (let alone a solution), but because we have no idea if they even have a need or any desire for it.

Whereas selling to a fully aware audience is simple. They know what they want. All that remains is to find out if they need it now and can afford it. It's the simplest sell in the world. Needless to say, an aware audience is what most advertisers aim for, and that's certainly the case with the example ad for our bookshop owner.

8 Short copy ads

How long should an ad be?

How many words do you need to sell a product? The answer is obvious: as many as it takes. However, this question comes up a lot in copywriting groups (and even more so when it comes to content writing - but that's mostly for SEO reasons - see Appendix B - SEO).

It's also often said that the length of an ad depends on the price of the product being sold (i.e., if it's expensive, then it's going to need more words). Both observations are true and untrue, and that's where audience awareness is useful: once you understand how aware your audience is likely to be, you'll have a better idea of how long any piece of copy for that audience and what you're selling should be.

For example: if I'm fully aware of the product I want to buy, and the only thing I'm interested in is the price, the copy could be as short as one sentence - even if the thing I was after was as expensive as a private jet.

Trust

Whilst this is true, there's one element we have yet to talk about. Trust. If I'm in the market to buy a Boeing 777x, described as "The World's Largest Twin Engine Jet" - a major selling point, then any ad put out by Boeing is all the trust I'd need - they could write "Boeing 777x on long-term lease with 0% down. Call Today" and I probably would - assuming I were in the market to buy one.

But if the ad came from some other company and said something like "Cheapest Plane Deals On The Planet", I'd need a lot more convincing. For example - I'd want to know if I could trust them; how long they'd been around; if the deal was tied in any way to Boeing's after-sales service; what their company financials were like; what guarantees they had; if they were Boeing approved; and so on.

It soon becomes obvious that a single sentence ad is not going to sell it to me. In fact, I'm going to want a whole lot more including a glossy fancy brochure with all the stats and facts included.

I'm probably going to want a face-to-face meeting with not just any old sales rep, but perhaps a vice-president of the company (VP's are two a penny in the corporate world, but the status implied by the label still holds value for most people).

Objections

Every one of the things I've just described is an objection. Objections are the holy grail of copywriters. Without them, we know nothing about our audience no matter how aware they are of what we're selling (there's a lot more about this coming later, and also in Appendix A - Objection handling).

Given what we've just learned, how do we know for sure whether a short copy ad will work, and what do we mean by short copy ad anyway?

Here's an example of one:

"Whilst it's true that many people suffer from hair loss problems, there is now a simple solution that restores a full head of hair in less than 6 weeks guaranteed, and best of all, it's affordable for everyone (not just Elton John). Call today on #xxx-xxx-xxxx to find out how you can get your full head of hair back affordably with our interest free payment plans."

That's 66 words. But it's still nowhere near as short as the vast majority of ads seen online on platforms such as Google.

I just searched Google for 'hair loss treatment' and the average ad length was 20 words. The top ad also had some extra snippets included, but even with those, the total number of words was less than 60.

I also searched for 'Boeing 777 for sale' and similar queries including 747, jumbo jet, but there were zero ads. Since we're in the middle of a financial airline meltdown (due to COVID-19), perhaps that's not surprising, so I tried 'private jets for sale' instead.

Two ads came up. The first was for Flexjets, the second was for NetJets. They contained 45 and 44 words respectively. Here's the text (copied and pasted as is - typos and grammatical errors included):

FLEXJET Ad:
Flexjet Official Site - Private Aviation At Its Best Enjoy the Freedom to Fly Your Way. Own Only as Much As You Need. Learn More. Welcome to Private Jet Travel at Its Best. Explore Our Aircraft Collection. Schedule A Consultation. Speak With A Expert. Request Information.

NETJETS ad:
Private Jet For Sale - Access 750 Jets Worldwide

Every Jet Is Spotlessly Clean and Stocked With the Amenities You Prefer. We Provide an Easier, More Reliable, and Luxurious Travel Experience. Unmatched Service. Highest Safety Standards. Travel On Your Terms. 120+ Countries. 24/7 Availability.

Admittedly, Google forces its advertisers to write ads in small chunks of characters, so it's not easy to write meaningful sentences, but nevertheless, it's a copywriter's job to do exactly that.

The two landing pages these ads send visitors to are similar. They are both dominated by images with short paragraphs. The call to action (or CTA) on both ads uses a form to collect details so prospects can schedule a call with an expert.

Let's take a look at the wording used in the CTA:

FLEXJET landing page:
Let's begin your ascent. Schedule a private consultation and experience Red Label for yourself at Flexjet House in London. Or, call us at #xx-xxx-xxxx and let us personalise a private travel programme unlike anything you've ever experienced.

NETJETS landing page:
Call today for a personal consultation with one of our private aviation experts.

Which do you think is better? It doesn't matter. Our opinion is irrelevant unless we're their target audience - although we can still put ourselves in their shoes if we know something about them.

Flexjet's CTA is romantic. It uses language that feels more aligned with its audience (we get that from the word "ascent"). Whereas Netjet gets straight to the point, but uses a couple of adjectives to suggest exclusivity (more about exclusivity coming up in chapter 9, Appendix F, and the glossary).

We can take it for granted that these two companies know their numbers. They know who their audience is, they know what's worked in the past, and they know what to expect from their ads.

In other words, there's a good chance both ads work equally as well. The fact that the two landing pages are so similar, suggests they researched not just their market, but their competitors too.

Get into the habit of reading ads and landing pages as often as you can. And remember, the more expensive the click, the more likely it is that the copy was written by a professional (the more a company spends on advertising, the more they have to lose - and that's a huge responsibility, especially when it comes to shareholders, so these companies will only hire the best copywriters).

Display ads

As well as standard search ads, display ads are everywhere too. The main platform is Google, with the Google Display Network but there are plenty of others too (and many sites operate their own service).

There is a strong comparison with traditional print advertising here. In newspapers, the search ad equivalent is called Classified and the display network uses the term Display.

Generally speaking, search or classified ads are text only, whereas display ads are image or graphics based.

You'd be forgiven for thinking that the Google Display Network is all about images though (even though that's what tends to come to mind). It's rare for an image without text to sell anything. This is good news for us, because if there's one thing we do better than anyone else, it's finding the right words to fit our audience (whatever image is used in the ad).

What should a short copy ad consist of?

Headline

Every ad should have a headline. In most countries, people read from left to right, top to bottom, so the first thing we're likely to see is either the headline or an image at the top of the page.

Often though we're attracted by an image no matter where it is on the page (and especially if it dominates the page).

If it's the image that attracts us, in almost all cases, we tend to go to the top of the page to find out more, and that means the headline.

What should a headline do?

The purpose of a headline is to both attract us and get us to read the first sentence. If it fails to do that, then it fails completely. The simplest way of achieving this is to set the headline up as a loop.

The idea of a loop is that a question is asked that compels the reader to find the answer. It also influences the reader to believe that the only way of finding the answer is to continue reading.

Every loop starts with an open element. This point in the loop is called an 'open loop', and that's just what the best headlines do.

When the answer is revealed, the loop is closed, and unless another loop has been opened in between, there is a chance the reader will stop reading (the question has been answered, nothing else to know).

For content writers, the most common headline open loop starts with the words: "How to...." Having read that, the reader is now clear that by continuing to read, they will get the answer.

For copywriters, it's the same thing, the only difference being that the final loop can only be closed with a call to action, typically to buy a product or fill in a form (but also sometimes to click a link to find out more if the copy is part of a sales funnel).

Another common form of open loop headline is the use of intrigue or curiosity. There are countless examples online, many can be found in embedded ad sections within major sites (national newspaper sites are a good source). If you see a headline that makes you want to find out more (for whatever reason), it's an example of an open loop and may involve any number of different variations.

A headline can be a statement or a question. Any headline that is a question is an automatic open loop (humans love answering questions, or finding out the answer to a question).

Statement style headlines include our first example ("How to...") but also include rhetorical questions (simple to spot as they rarely end with a question mark. E.g., "Why did the chicken cross the road...") as well as those that imply an article contains the answer (e.g., "Top Ten Tips To...").

If you ever get stuck for headline ideas, open Google and search for anything. Every search result has a headline. If the search includes ads, realise that each of those ads contains a headline written by a copywriter (or should have been) and is being paid for by someone.

Anchoring

Another common factor used in headlines (especially short copy ads) is anchoring. If I ask you right now "when did you last see a red car?", I force your brain to go into memory search. You cannot help yourself. Red cars have now been anchored in your head, and you will be thinking about red cars for a while before your brain decides it's had enough (but the idea of "red cars" may come back randomly (or because you see one) over the next few days. That is anchoring.

The most common use of anchoring is pricing though. If I tell you that the price of an average new red car is £12,000, that becomes the new anchor for the price of any red car (for you).

So if I later tell you that you can now get a new ABC car in red for just £8,000, your brain immediately tells you it's a bargain. And if I also say the deal goes away in 24 hours, I've given you a reason for the cheaper price (you might think: "this is some kind of sale, and of course, it can't last forever, because this looks like a real bargain").

Common short copy ad headlines go something like this: "Today Only. £269 Men's Bikes Now £159. Act Fast." In just a few words we've anchored the prospect's mind at £269 for a bike, then compared that to the sale price of £159. If we removed the pricing anchor, this ad would only have a fraction of the power.

Anchoring is not just restricted to colour and price though. We can anchor people on anything. For example, suppose we need people to believe that dieting is hard, but our diet (the one we're selling in an ad) is easy. We could use a headline like this: "People Say Dieting Is Hard, But Not Those On The NEW XYZ Diet. Start Today. Lose Weight."

Short copy ad content

Every ad also contains some body text. For short copy ads such as those displayed in search engines, the number of characters is fixed (at around 90 characters per line, with up to 2 lines - and remember, that's 180 characters, not words).

This is hugely restrictive, and means we have to get creative when it comes to messaging. This is a good thing when it comes to learning to be a copywriter. Brevity is at the heart of good copy.

It's often said that if we can't explain at least the basic outline of anything in a single sentence, then we probably don't understand it. Think about this when talking with a prospect, if they're unable to tell you in a single sentence what it is their 'thing' does and why it matters, then you automatically know they need help.

We don't have the same restrictions for display ads, but we do have a restriction on ad size, so nothing really changes. The message has to be to the point. If the reader doesn't know what it is being advertised, they will not hang around to find out.

A great exercise to do every day is to pick some object in your office or home and write a short copy ad. Start doing this from now on until it becomes a habit. Eventually, you'll be able to do it in your head without thinking. This will help you enormously when presenting to prospective clients (if you can come up with an ad on the spot about something they're selling, their confidence in you will increase).

9 Long copy ads

Ads come in all shapes and sizes, but one of those sizes has been used more or less since advertising became a thing, and that is long copy ads. These are primarily used in the direct response marketing industry.

Before the internet there were three prime channels for these types of ads:

1. Mail
2. Display ads
3. Infomercials

All these channels still survive, although the display ad version is not seen very often these days.

To give you an idea of how big the direct response marketing industry is, the US postal service handled 76 billion pieces of marketing mail in 2018 (the industry was estimated to be worth $44bn a year later in 2019 and continues to grow today).

With figures like that, you can be certain you're entering a huge industry with plenty of opportunity as a new professional copywriter.

Now we also have the internet as a channel (some would say the perfect channel), long copy ads are increasing at a faster rate than ever, but it requires skill to pen a 10,000 word ad, and that's where this chapter comes in.

What is a long copy ad?

There is no definition for a long copy ad other than it contains more than a few paragraphs of text - typically at least one page long (how big the page is doesn't matter, but we're talking about anything at least as big as a standard book page).

The reason to differentiate between short and long copy ads comes down to purpose. A short copy ad is there to get someone to make a quick decision (e.g., click a link or call a number).

Long copy ads are there to sell by disseminating as much information as possible to get the reader motivated enough to take some kind of major action (i.e., part with their cash) by the time they've finished reading.

What sorts of things are sold with long copy ads?

The same sorts of things that are sold with short copy ads. It's often said that higher priced items need more effort to sell, and whilst that is generally true, the difference between long and short copy ads is not usually about the cost of things.

Books are sold using both long and short copy ads. Major luxury items are sold using both types of ad as well. But what a long copy ad is very good at doing (or should be if it's to be profitable) is build a small desire into a large desire.

The length of any long copy ad depends entirely on how long that process takes (i.e., conversion from interested to sold) when applied to a specific target audience. If it takes 10 seconds, then we don't need a long copy ad. If it's going to take 30 minutes then we do.

How do we know how long it will take? We don't. This comes down to targeting and awareness levels of who we're targeting. More on that in the prospecting section (see chapter 11).

Let's start at the top

We'll now go through a long copy ad from start to end, section by section (you'll see examples shortly). Some sections are vital like the headline, others are not - like the preheadline, which is where we'll start - right at the top:

Preheadline

Not all copy has a preheadline (a short piece of text shown just above the headline), but when it does, it's there to presell the headline or open a loop.

It's especially abundant in long copy ads, and helps get another benefit across without shouting it quite as loudly as the headline does (usually by using a smaller font size).

Does your copy need a preheadline? You'll soon know because you'll realise you need to say just a little bit more before readers get to your perfectly worded headline. Often, this is something added after the main copy has been written.

Headline

A headline is a headline right? We already know a lot about headlines, but when it comes to long copy ads, headlines become just that little bit more important. Why? Because they've got to persuade someone not just to read the first sentence, but to invest a lot of time into what is obviously going to be an extended reading session.

They know this from just looking at the condensed text of a typical long copy ad. And if the text is well spaced with plenty of subheadings and other areas of interest, well, it's going to cover a lot more pages, so there's the 'thud factor' to take into account.

NOTE: the thud factor is a metaphor of the sound made when something large (and therefore by implication, important because of its weight) hits the ground.

From an online perspective this isn't so obvious at the start, but most people are used to seeing how small the scroll bar becomes when presented with a long page of content, and after a scroll or two it becomes glaringly obvious that the page they're about to read is not going to be completed in a matter of seconds (or even minutes).

Most of this thinking happens subconsciously. Our DNA dictates that anything that involves time, risk, or cost, needs to be evaluated long before it reaches our consciousness - and if it does get that far, it's generally too late because the reader will have already got bored and moved on to the next thing that gets their attention.

So our headline has to attract them, engage them, and then hook them into wanting to explore whatever it promises - without them having to consciously think about it - or worse, having to figure out what it means.

This leads us to another difference between short copy ads and long copy ads. Headlines that work on intrigue alone won't cut it. They need to be meatier, and they need to be clearer, but above all, they need to talk to the EXACT audience they're targeting (not least because every other audience will get bored fast).

As a general rule, long copy ad headlines should answer these three questions:

1. What is it?
2. Who is it for?
3. Why does it matter?

Here's one from a subsidiary of Agora: "Seven Keys to Seven Figures - How to Achieve Independence... on Your Terms."

What is it? Something to do with money, and in particular millionaire status money.
Who is it for? Anyone who wants financial independence.
Why does it matter? Because you can achieve this "on your terms."

From that headline, we know this isn't going to be a short read because it's going to be discussing seven keys on how to do it (and also because anyone who ever wanted to achieve millionaire status on their terms would be doing it already if it was so easy).

Here's another (this one from the Motley Fool website): "Could this FTSE 100 industry giant be one of the best shares to buy now?"

What is it? Some kind of investment.

Who is it for? Anyone interested in buying shares.
Why does it matter? Because it sounds like it's going to make us a lot of money.

Both of these headlines (and they are typical for this type of market) are followed by a lot of text and data, but they are actually just the tips of long and involved sales funnels that ultimately lead to a number of offers (some of which cost many thousands of dollars).

Once someone has been exposed to these headlines and has taken action, the copywriters know exactly where to take them next on their journey. Everything builds, point by point, until the desire that was there at the start has blossomed into a sale.

Get it right, and long copy ads can produce millions of dollars. Get it wrong, and it becomes an expensive mistake. This is why everything is tested before any real money is spent.

It works the same way for most industries, the movie industry being a typical example, where only one in ten films is a blockbuster, a few break even, and the rest lose money.

Control

This is why something called a "control" matters. To test, you must start somewhere, and that somewhere (i.e., your ad copy) becomes the first control. If another version of the ad beats the original ad (in terms of conversions), that new version of the ad becomes the new control.

When it comes to finding your first prospects, this knowledge (of control pieces) is your best new friend (more on this in the prospecting section).

Practice writing headlines every day. You will benefit greatly, but don't just write one headline for a product, write numerous headlines for the same product. Think about the big idea behind each headline (i.e., has it got one big idea? And if so, are you sticking to just the one or muddling it up with other big ideas).

Whilst it's easy to find short copy headline examples on the internet, long copy ads are considerably rarer. This is because these headlines are mostly used after some other action has been performed, the most obvious of which is after someone has opted in to something of less value by way of a lead magnet.

Set up a separate free email account and use it to opt in to everything you come across, then wait for the spam to arrive and see what you get. It will uncover a plethora of ideas and give you a good insight into what's going on right now and what products and services are being sold using long copy sales ads.

The subheadline

Sometimes it's necessary to add a subheadline. This is a sentence or two of text just below the headline, and usually written using a smaller font (but still larger than the body copy font).

Like the preheadline, it's there to add something extra (a feature, advantage, or benefit) to enhance the headline a little further (whether you choose to use a feature, advantage, or benefit depends on the awareness level of the target audience - the whole point about awareness being that it's a journey of discovery, so the less aware people are, the more we need to step back and explain things).

The lede (also known as lead)

Every piece of copy has a lede (or lead or leader - see Lede in the Glossary). It's the section that follows the headline (and any subheadline).

If you've got someone past the headline, then you'll need to do everything you can to keep them reading, and that means having a big idea (see chapter 7).

The lede is where that big idea is expanded upon (assuming it was touched on in the headline).

A lede can be anything from a single sentence to a few paragraphs - whatever it takes to make it clear this is something special and what follows is worthy of the reader's attention.

If the lede fails, the copy fails. This cannot be emphasized enough. However, when a lede is written well, what follows it can be less than perfect and yet still keep the reader's attention (novels and films often feel like this, with an explosive start, a boring middle section, and an explosive, emotional, or surprising end that makes up for it).

Don't let that put you off making everything explosive, emotional, or surprising though. All sections of copy should keep the reader hooked and wanting to read on, no need to shoot your copy in the foot by getting lazy when it could have been so much better.

Lede example

Before you read the following example of a lede, I need to set the scene: The product being offered is a pen. The big idea is that this pen can be used for both analog and digital writing. It's the world's first multi-surface pen.

Here's the preheadline:

"Introducing the world's first multi-surface pen..."

Here's the headline:
"At last, the pen you've always wanted, but could never find"

Here's the subheadline:

"Use on paper, tablet, phone, laptop, anywhere..."

And here's the lede:

"The AnoDigi Pen is the world's first multi-surface pen, patented by master inventor Reginald Pennin."

This lede is a complete fiction of course, but did it pique your interest? If you could buy a pen that wrote on all surfaces, whether they are analog like paper, or digital like a smart phone, would you buy it - or at least want to know more, and if so, what else would you want to know?

That's what a lede does. Pulls you into the story so fast, you forget you're reading an ad at all. Where the preheadline, headline, and subheadline get your attention, the lede gets your engagement.

The body

After the lede comes the body text. This can consist of many segments, the order of which depends (as always) on the awareness level of the audience you're targeting.

The journey

Long copy gives us room to tell the whole story. If the headline and lede are right, readers expect nothing less, they're with us all the way provided we give them what they want (not what we want - that will happen anyway if we get the first part right).

If our audience knows what they want and are ready to buy from us right now, long copy is a waste of time. All objections have been handled. All they need is a "Buy Now" button.

If they know what they want and are looking for the best supplier, we're going to need more than a buy now button, that much is obvious. But what more do we need?

Let's continue with the pen example. Are we the manufacturer? If the answer is yes, then it would seem that's all we need to say. It's enough to know that they're buying from the most trusted source there is.

But suppose they believe they may be able to get it cheaper elsewhere? Telling them they can buy it from any of our licenced stockists might be a good idea, but do we have licenced stockists in the first place? (Most small manufacturers are delighted to let anyone become a stockist if they're willing to pay up front - licence or no licence).

Do we explain that they can't buy it cheaper elsewhere? That would damage our relationship with stockists, exceedingly bad for business.

Which means if we have stockists to sell our pen we cannot burn those bridges, so how can we sell direct? The answer is we shouldn't if we want to keep those relationships strong.

The next scenario is that we are one of many suppliers of the pen. How can we differentiate ourselves? The obvious answer is to discount it. But that reduces our profit (and setting an expectation that everything we sell is discounted - is that a good position to take in a crowded market? Not usually, it becomes a race to the bottom by effectively inviting our competitors to follow suit)

Value

But one angle we can adopt is to add value. That way we can sell the pen at its full recommended price. We also win trust (because only the most trusted sources sell at RRP - it's a perception that the business doesn't need to make sales to succeed, therefore the business will be around for a long time - which means they will be there for us if something goes wrong).

What does adding value mean? In the world of internet marketing, it means adding bonuses, but in the real world of bricks and mortar businesses and tangible products, it means adding something genuinely useful to the purchaser of the product, so in our example of a pen, it means the bonus MUST be directly connected with the pen

92

AND its solving of our audience's problem (the reason why they want this pen).

One added value could be the addition of refills. It might be a guide to calligraphy if our pen is capable of being used for that purpose (and since the claim is that you'll never need another pen, then perhaps it has changeable nibs, which means we could also add an extra nib or two if they buy through us).

By going through the process of understanding our audience, we also now have a new big idea to think about: "You'll never need another pen ever again." This may be the idea we use for a further campaign, or it may be something we can add to our current campaign. The more we dig into our ideal customer, the more this sort of thing happens (and the more we dig, the less likely it is our competitors are likely to keep up).

The first paragraph after the lede needs to expand on the lede further. We must never lose sight of what we're promising with each unfolding paragraph. Here's the lede again:

"The AnoDigi Pen is the world's first multi-surface pen, patented by master inventor Reginald Pennin."

And here are the next two paragraphs based on what we've just been discussing - our audience, their needs and perceptions:

"What do we mean by a 'multi-surface' pen? Suppose you're taking notes at a seminar and your pen runs out of ink. What do you do? Scrabble around for another pen,

ask the person sitting next to you if they have a spare one, panic?

"You won't need to with the AnoDigi Pen because you'll never run out of ink - digital ink that is. The AnoDigi comes complete with its own AnoDigi Paper^tm (as well as being able to write on almost any type of digital writing device)."

Still interested? I hope so. I can't wait for someone to invent this product. I want one already, which means I'm in a great position to start writing copy about it.

What I've done is take the reader from what the product IS (a pen) to a journey of discovery.

We have created a story about where one might find this magical device being used. As you can see from the above ad, we've taken our readers into an imaginary seminar room where they're now reliving the experience of taking notes and running out of ink (i.e., they now have a problem that needs fixing).

The reader is part of the story and on the journey to owning a pen. The sentences are short, punchy, simple, but above all, to the point.

Are they ready to buy from us yet? Again, it depends on their awareness. If they were fully aware, they already knew the product existed, they were just undecided whether to buy it from us or not. They already knew the pen came with a digital writing pad, so most of our copy was, for them, a waste of time.

But what about an audience who, whilst being aware there was a solution, didn't know about our solution? This ad fits them to a tee. They know they need a new pen, but now they've discovered something that is so much more than a pen - it not only fixes their problem right now, it fixes them for life too.

Here's the next paragraph of the ad:

"AnoDigi Paper^{tm} is a new kind of smart paper. It feels like paper to write on, you can store it flat, or roll it up, but best of all, it never runs out!"

We've just added another feature and supported that feature with a clear benefit (like the pen, the paper never runs out either) as well as an advantage (it is unique), plus, we have added another big idea ("a pen that never runs out").

As you know, most successful ads are based on a big idea, and that big idea is described over and over throughout the copy in different ways. This keeps the reader focused on one thing - the thing that sets the product apart from everything else.

If you look at our big ideas so far, we have:

1. Combines analog and digital (writes on real paper and smart paper)
2. You'll never need another pen (no more costs)
3. Never run out of ink (or paper) again

At this point we could reengineer our big ideas by combining them under a new working title, for example "A pen for life." Having penned that, my immediate thoughts turn to education and charities.

Suppose some of the profits of this product were to go to charity? Suppose that charity was set up to help educate those for whom education was not easy to get? Now we have a pen that's not only for our life, it's for everyone else's too.

And that gives us another advantage over our competitors. If our solution seeking prospect hears that by buying this pen, they will also be helping others, it not only positions our company as one that cares (and legitimises it if we include the charities logo and a statement from the chairperson), but also adds a compelling reason to buy from us (if they appreciate the work that the supported charity does).

If we were to go for that angle, it also means our audience demographic has just changed slightly. Let's add another paragraph:

"But this not only never runs out for you, it never runs out for those in need too. When you purchase an AnoDigi Pen through us, 20% of the profit goes direct to the AnoDigi Foundation's work with [insert charity] helping pay for educational materials for those who need it most."

At this point in the copy, we've just transitioned from story to CTA. We could end the copy here with something like this:

"To help make our world a better place (so we all never run out of pens, ink, or paper again), hit the Buy Now button below and we'll ship your AnoDigi Pen within 24 hours to anywhere in the world."

By ending it early, we've really created a short copy ad, but that's not the point. We can expand on this ad for as long as we want if we believe it will help sell more. Only testing will confirm this of course. An ad should always be exactly as long as it takes to make a sale (or get the reader to take action on the CTA) and no longer (regardless of labels like short or long copy - they're really just guides to differentiate between different ways of putting ads together depending on how much convincing the ad's target audience needs).

It's rare for brand new groundbreaking products to appear (most new products are copies of old products with very few differences), so on the whole, we'll find we're mostly writing copy for audiences who are aware of both the problem and solution. But where truly new products do appear, long copy is almost always required.

One such product was the iPhone. We all knew what a phone was, and we all knew what the internet was, but up to that point, we'd never connected a phone with the internet (let alone apps). Apple had a lot of work to do to convince the world that it needed yet another new gadget.

They had already lost a lot of money in the 90's marketing the Newton (a handheld app device), and many other originators and copycats had done the same and failed. So the idea of trying it again would put most investors off.

But Apple had (and still has) deep pockets and thrived on their original strategy (and ad slogan) of Think Different™. So that's what they did.

If you search YouTube for "first official iPhone ad" you will come across their original 30 second "Hello" TV ad that announced that something called an "iPhone" was coming soon.

It's a clever ad. It features a whole bunch of well known actors (using snippets from famous films) saying "Hello" and featuring phones through the ages.

It tells the story of old to new, taking us on a brief history of the phone, and letting us know that the next major phone update is about to happen - and we're going to get our greedy, inquisitive little hands on it soon.

The ad associated the iPhone with what's already existing (helping us to adjust to the revolution that's about to occur, thus making it not so frightening), and also associated it with the most popular actors of the past and present.

After watching that ad, search for "iPhone 1 - Steve Jobs MacWorld keynote in 2007" and you'll come across the full 80 minute keynote on the iPhone. How many words do you think were in that keynote?

If we take the most conservative estimate of 100 spoken words a minute, the transcription of Steve Jobs' keynote would have been 8000 words (and many images).

Was it necessary? Jobs thought so. He knew the most important part of any sales process was demonstration. If you can demonstrate something, it beats every other way of selling.

The proof of Jobs' strategy resulted in the world's first $trillion company. Not bad for a two word strategy - Think Different™.

Show don't tell

This simple rule says it all. If we can write copy in such a way that prospects imagine themselves involved in the story, then we have not only demonstrated to them what it would be like to own this thing we're selling, we've also shown them it's possible.

Showing instead of telling is simple to do using video or graphics, but slightly harder using just the written word (see Rule 12 - Show don't tell).

For copy, it really means adding benefits to every feature in such a way as to encourage prospects to use their imagination.

We want them to start experiencing what this product will do for them once they own it. We want them to see themselves using this product in real life. The more clearly we can describe the experience, and the closer we can get that experience to mirror what they want, the more their desire will increase.

Desire and passion

I talked a lot about desire in the introduction. It's time to expand on that, and in particular, connect it to its close companion: passion. But before we do that, we need to revisit needs and wants.

We looked briefly at needs and wants in chapter 5, here's the important part when it comes to the connection between needs, wants, desire, and passion: a need is something we must have. A want is something we don't need.

A desire is the motivation we must have to get what we need. For example, if we need to eat, we eat, but if we have no desire to eat, we eventually become ill and starve. This makes the motivation to eat extremely strong.

Yet even with a seemingly inherent desire like eating, some people have no desire to do so, and when that happens, no amount of external persuasion seems to work (it takes a great deal of time and many different types of intervention to cure an eating disorder - ask any dieter).

In short, without desire, nothing happens. For our short and long copy ads, at least a spark of desire (or some close connection to it) must be present for the ad to have any effect.

What a good ad does is increase that spark of desire to the point at which the prospect is motivated enough to take the action we're asking them to do.

And that's the purpose of the body copy of any long copy ad. Where the headline gets attention and the lede gets engagement, the body copy increases desire.

But we can go one step further with our copy. If we can increase the desire so much it turns into passion, the product will be as good as sold. And when passion takes over, irrationality steps in (it's also how villains operate, so take care with this).

Here's the definition of desire via Google: "a strong feeling of wanting to have something or wishing for something to happen."

And here's the definition of passion: "strong and barely controllable emotion."

Note the difference: desire is a strong feeling, whereas passion is a barely controllable emotion. Which do you think sells more?

Building desire

You only need the tiniest amount of initial desire to take someone from mildly interested to rabid fan, but achieving that will always be the hardest thing to do in marketing (getting attention is easy in comparison).

Furthermore, that tiniest bit of desire is often not even seemingly connected with whatever it is you're selling.

All our desires are connected with our childhood. As our minds slowly fill with different impressions of the world mapped out by the many emotions we accrue along the way, so the associations between the objects and people we mix with in life combine with the feelings we get from those associations and how those feelings compare with, and then invoke feelings from our past.

For example, being driven in a car as a child may end with an exciting trip to the seaside, along with a bundle of extras such as ice cream, fish and chips, sun, sea, and sand castles. These are going to make a strong impression and leave you with a good feeling about journeys (especially car journeys).

If later in life you happen to be looking for a new car, then any associations you make with the seaside and car journeys are going to trigger good emotions in you, and from there on in, your desire to own a new car is going to increase.

If I'm the person writing the ad targeted to sell you a new car, then the stronger I can make that association, the more desire you'll get. At any point along the way, I can also start introducing more practical things - e.g., "the commute is going to feel a whole lot better with this model because of the panoramic sunroof" (any association with words connected with your good seaside experiences, however remote those words may be, are all part of the triggering system - i.e., "sun" roof).

I could also point out "the fold down tables in the back of the car where you can eat fish and chips in complete comfort whatever the weather" and you'll be taken another step closer to a sale.

Step by step

Just like any exciting adventure, your body copy takes the reader one small step at a time towards the sale, building feature by feature combined with relevant benefits until the desire becomes so strong, the reader becomes part of the story.

Feature list

A good place to start with your body copy is by writing down a list of all the features of the product or service you're selling.

A feature is anything a product or service IS, HAS or DOES. Whilst every product or service being sold is there to fix a problem, each feature represents one part of that fix, so if you feel stuck trying to figure out your feature list, start by thinking about the problems the product or service was created to fix.

Let's take the example of a car. If we were told to write some copy to sell a car, where would we start?

Our first thoughts would probably be: "What sort of car is it? What make? What model?" These are all things we need to know of course, but once we have those, we need to know what differentiates this car from all the others.

Those differentiators are the features we're after. We call them 'advantages', and they are part of the FAB framework (see Appendix C - FAB).

Without knowing the advantages, our features are going to be like every other car. E.g., "Has an engine", "is a vehicle", "has four wheels", and whilst all these matter, they will not increase desire.

However, there are some features that whilst being fairly normal, are not present on every car. These features DO matter, just not as much as those that we consider unique or rare on a car.

These might include things such as electric windows, heated seats, sunroof, satnav, automatic parking system, etc. Many cars have these things, but not ALL cars.

From this we can see we're going to need to categorise our feature list into standard features, non-standard features, and unique features.

Feature order

Our body copy is going to use these features to build desire, so you'd be forgiven for thinking we'd start with standard features, add non-standard features, and end with unique features. After all, it feels like it would make sense to write it that way.

The problem is, standard features are boring. If we have any desire to buy a car at all, we need to be hit with something amazing from the outset. To be told it has an Automatic Braking System (ABS) or Power Assisted Steering (PAS) is not going to do it (but they still matter).

So how about starting with nonstandard features? Similar problem. It's nice to know our car will beep loudly if we're about to reverse into a wall, but that's what we might expect from a car with sensors (i.e., nothing new = same old same old).

But what if our car has NO new features? Nothing unique to make it stand out? Just standard features (e.g., a bottom of the range model). It means we need to get creative.

One way to do that is lateral thinking. Ask questions such as "what are the elements that every car must have by law?" One answer might be 'safety equipment'.

Since all cars must pass the minimum safety standards required by law (or they won't be allowed on the forecourt), we just need to get creative with words:

"The New [insert make and model] comes with every safety feature you need as standard, protecting you and your family while you enjoy trips to the seaside."

It doesn't matter that every other car has to pass them too (and therefore has the same features), by highlighting them, our car becomes the standard (i.e., we position our car as the standard every other manufacturer must conform to).

This works because we become the first manufacturer to put it into print by way of advertising.

Ethics and morals

Is it moral to do this? In this example, yes - because we're telling the truth (it's true our car has all the standard safety equipment). But if we were villains, we'd use every trick in the book to associate a product we were selling with anything at all that gets it sold.

We can choose to be a villain and do the same thing of course, but someone somewhere will most likely spot it, and the reputation damage will be huge (so regardless of whether you're a villain, always be truthful if you want a long and sustainable business).

But what is truth anyway? Anything that is not a lie. If our car passes all standard security tests, then that's as good a feature as any other to advertise if no one else has used that as their Unique Selling Point or Proposition (USP) before.

First to market

When we announce that something is available to the world for the first time (be it a product or feature), it's called being 'first to market'. What's interesting in this example of a car with standard safety features is that the USP we're using to sell it is not 'first to market', it's the fact that we're advertising it this way that is.

Volvo's advertising campaigns of the 1990's used this angle with their famous 'Jaws' style advert "Cages Save Lives."

What we've done is create something unique out of something ordinary. You can apply this to any product or service where there's no obvious differentiator.

Commodities

All commodities suffer this same problem of being ordinary or 'everyday' (whether it's beers, beans, or bacon). This is why the most common word in advertising is NEW. It's our get-out clause when stuck for something new to write. We just use the word "new" itself, and the public accepts it because no one ever bought the "old" version if the new one was labelled NEW (with a few classic exceptions such as Coca-Cola after their New Coke campaign flopped - they even tried Coke II, but that failed too).

Nonstandard features

It's harder to get creative when it comes to nonstandard features though. There's more likelihood that those features, which were once first to market, are still front of mind for many people.

For example, 4 x 4 vehicles. They've been around for 120+ years (invented 1893), yet they're still nonstandard. But get creative and you can come up with numerous ways of making 4 x 4 sound interesting again (and by doing so, implying uniqueness again).

To do this, use the 10 in 10 method. Set a timer for 10 minutes, and start writing down everything you can think of that a 4 x 4 vehicle can do that a normal vehicle can't. We set the timer so it forces our brain to come up with ideas. It's a race and most of us are programmed to try to win races (from our schooling etc.).

Once the timer stops, it doesn't mean you have to stop coming up with ideas, it just gives you some sense of closure (which is what we need to motivate us to do something - think of it as the pot of gold at the end of the rainbow).

NOTE: This is not easy. Coming up with a list of 10 things to do with something is usually simple up to around the 5 or 6 item mark, but then it becomes much harder. However, do this often and your brain will reprogram itself over time.

Here's my list of features that differentiate a 4 x 4 vehicle from an ordinary one:
1. Drive on the roughest of roads
2. Added safety in the rain
3. Perceived greater status
4. Faster acceleration
5. Faster stopping
6. Higher ride (for greater vision)
7. Heavier towing capacity
8. Rarely get stuck in mud
9. Improved slow speed handling
10. Ability to climb and descend steeper slopes

What we've done is create a further 10 features and some benefits out of one original feature ('four-wheel drive'). This allows us to write copy that highlights those features and benefits without even needing to refer to the original 4 x 4 feature at all.

"Imagine a car so safe it can drive on snow, in the rain, up and down the steepest of roads, slow or fast, give you more vision than most other cars on the road, and all without missing a beat. That's the new [insert make and model]."

We can sell a whole bunch of common features with ease this way by describing only the benefits.

Benefits

As we learnt earlier, a feature is the IS, HAS, or DOES of a product or service. A car IS a vehicle, a pen IS a tool used for writing. A car HAS an engine, a pen HAS an ink reservoir. What a car DOES is travel from A to B. What a pen DOES is enable ink to be transferred to paper.

Features matter, but without being told their benefits we have very little idea if they'll be useful to us or not.

I see this everywhere - lists of features with almost zero benefits explained. It's a clear indicator of where I can be of service to someone as a copywriter. I KNOW I can improve their business if I come across copy that is heavy on features but light on benefits (remember this one paragraph when you're ready to go prospect hunting).

Benefits are defined by a single word: WHY? Why should I get this? Why is this useful to me? Why should I get this now? Why should I buy this from you? Why should I pay you so much money for this?

NOTE: I'm sure you can think of a lot more questions, especially when someone is pressuring you into buying something - e.g., why should I listen, let alone trust you?

Going back to my 10 in 10 list for a 4 x 4 car, let's explore each item. I'll add a benefit after each one in quotes so you can see how it might look in an ad.

1. Drive on the roughest of roads: "Go on adventures to places other vehicles cannot reach"
2. Added safety in the rain: "Keep your family safe even when it's pouring down with rain"
3. Perceived greater status: "Lord it up in the community and watch the look on your neighbour's face" (some people consider this a benefit!)
4. Faster acceleration: "Overtake in safety"
5. Faster stopping: "Give cats an extra life" (this may be too subtle, it's also an attempt at humour, which I would avoid unless you're a professional comedian)
6. Higher ride (for greater vision): "See further down the road and even over hedges whilst going round corners"
7. Heavier towing capacity: "Get yourself a bigger caravan"
8. Rarely get stuck in mud: "Tow your friend's car out of the quagmire"
9. Improved slow speed handling: "Never worry about stalling the engine again"
10. Ability to climb and descend steeper slopes: "Now you can drive over the steepest of passes, see the scenery, and still feel safe even if it's icy"

You're not limited to one benefit per feature either (item #10 has 4 benefits). A great exercise to start doing on a daily basis is to look at the features of tools you're using and think about why you use them. What is it about those tools that makes you stick with them?

This is also a good time to start thinking about what it is with the tools you use that you would love to improve or change. It will help with your creativity, especially when it comes to getting clients (as you'll see later).

Objections

Every benefit is there to answer an objection (because every objection is there to stop a sale).

A great way to think about the journey you're taking prospects on, and not just in the body of your copy, but in the copy as a whole, is the order of objections.

A newspaper journalist thinks in terms of story all the time. They know that newspapers only sell when the stories are good (that is, when they move people emotionally in some way).

Journalists' list

To do that, they assemble the facts (or at least, good journalists do). Think of this as a template you can use to create certain types of story-based copy. Here are those fact seeking questions (the order of the questions can be varied any way you like, and some of the answers can be inserted in more than one place, but this list follows a basic structure):

1. What happened?
2. Where did it happen?

3. Who was involved? (optional as far as copy is concerned, but often with long copy, it's important to mention the people involved if it makes sense to do so to win trust, authority, or proof)
4. Why did it happen?
5. What evidence is there? (answers can be inserted in multiple places if it makes sense to do so)
6. What was the outcome?
7. What are people saying about it? (again, answers can be inserted in multiple places if it makes sense to do so)
8. Could it happen again? (the use of fear to increase desire - optional but often highly effective - use with care)
9. Why does it matter? (this is usually the point of any article, so is rarely mentioned explicitly, instead, it's implied subtly throughout an article and usually based on the opinion of the writer, the publication, or the importance of the piece)
10. How can I find out more? (in journalism, this might include links to sources, in advertising, this would be the call to action)
11. When did it happen? (only relevant if it's important to the story and helps motivate a sale)

That first question ("what happened?") is the most important as far as journalists are concerned, but for copywriters, it really means "what is it? (or "what is it about?"). It answers the one thing everyone needs to know when they come into contact with any copy (if they have no idea what the copy is about, they are unlikely to have any incentive to read on, and also, if they do, and it turns out to be not what they expected or wanted, it can be costly in terms of pay-per-click rates and quality score for online ads).

If we take a non-story-based ad, the 'what is it?' is simple. Here's an example: "The world's first home wind farm." Let's turn that idea into a story-based ad. The story will revolve around a couple who decide to go for an alternative energy source and not rely on utility companies again. Here's the headline:

"Couple Take On Energy Companies And Win"

Here's the lede:

"When Mike and Doris Taylor got their highest ever energy bill earlier this year, they decided they'd had enough with paying exorbitant costs to utility companies, and started looking for alternative energy sources - ideally, ones they could run themselves."

Although we don't yet know what it is, we certainly know what it's about and we also know what happened (the #1 question). If we are in any way interested in alternative energy and/or perhaps generating it ourselves, we will want to continue reading.

Here's the next paragraph (the start of the body copy):

"After a quick search on Google, they discovered two things. The first was that they could own their own energy producing equipment without stumping up a small fortune, the second was that they could profit from it by plugging it into the national grid."

We now know "where" it happened (the #2 question) - at home - which implies it is something that could happen locally anywhere as well as something that anyone could do.

Let's look at the features we've added so far in just a couple of paragraphs:

1. A way of producing energy
2. The energy can be produced at home
3. The energy can earn money

You might think that all three items are benefits - and they would be if you already valued these features as something you wanted, but strictly speaking, they are features.

For example, a feature of steam powered engines. and later, motorised vehicles that replaced horses as a means of production gave us the term: horsepower. Up to that point, there was no 'horsepower'. There were just simply 'horses'.

We know the word horsepower is a FEATURE because that's what an engine DOES (produce horsepower). A benefit, on the other hand, is what something does FOR US.

To highlight why the world's engines were better than horses, the term horsepower became synonymous with how many horses could be replaced by the use of any particular engine.

The benefit of horsepower might be summed up like this: "if this one machine can replace six horses, I'm going to save a lot of money." We can go on to add more benefits to this - e.g., we might write copy like this: "I'll no longer need someone to look after the horses every day, feed them, or have to pay expensive vet bills either."

As the evolution of engines improved, so the number of 'horses' (in terms of power) increased and eventually the benefits of why horsepower mattered disappeared at the same rate horses did (at least, from a workhorse or transport point of view).

That is why we list our features as standard, non-standard, and unique. Everyone knows the benefits of standard features, not everyone knows the benefits of non-standard features, and almost no one knows the benefits of unique features (when a product is first released).

If we look at feature #2 from our list above: 'The energy can be produced at home', we know that since many things can be produced at home, it has no particular beneficial value over anything else that can be produced at home, so we're going to have to ensure this feature is enhanced by adding a benefit.

Here's the next paragraph of our copy:

"What was it Mike and Doris stumbled on? A DIY home wind farm. Within two weeks it was built and up and running supplying more than enough electricity to heat their house, and with the excess going direct to the national grid they were on to a nice little earner too."

The benefit we added was "earning them extra income" (i.e., what this feature "does for them").

Having said that, you're probably already objecting to some of the claims in this copy, and if that happened, then the flow of the story would have stopped for you. If any copy takes us out of the story and into a series of questions about it, we lose. So what's the first most likely objection here?

For me, it's the problem of wind. It's not always blowing, so how can it claim to supply 'more than enough electricity'? The objection would go something like this "that's not possible, what happens when there's no wind?"

We have a set of choices at this point. Find out the answer, ignore the objection, or edit the copy that's causing it - even to the point of deleting it. It all depends on the facts.

If it turns out we can have 24/7 electricity because the system includes storage batteries, then we need to rewrite the copy by handling the objection as it occurs.

If it turns out there's no 24/7 electricity, then we're probably better off dropping the claim altogether and looking for a new angle.

Let's imagine storage is part of the package. Here's the rewritten paragraph:

"What was it Mike and Doris stumbled on? A DIY home wind farm. Within two weeks it was built and up and running supplying more than enough electricity to heat their house with the built-in storage batteries allowing a 24/7 supply regardless of how much wind there was on any particular day. And with the excess electricity going direct to the national grid they were on to a nice little earner too."

Continuing with this copy and the next item (#3) in our journalist story template ("who was involved?"), well, we already know about Mike and Dorris, but what about the company they bought it from? Is it time to introduce them yet, or do we need to add more details?

To find out, let's go through the rest of the template:

Item #4 ("Why did it happen?") has already been covered (they were fed up paying utility companies and were looking for an alternative).

Item #5 ("What evidence is there?") definitely needs to be covered. All we have so far is that a DIY home wind farm is possible, and that someone has done it, but we don't know if that's true yet (there's no way to verify it). Many copywriters leave it at that (not because they have no further proof, but usually because the copywriter got lazy and couldn't be bothered to research it - this is another point to note when looking for prospects and reading their current ads - how can you improve them?).

Item #6 ("What was the outcome?") has been covered in that we've been told it was installed, working, and producing a profit in two weeks, but does it need more? Could we make it stronger?

Item #7 ("What are people saying about it?") is the perfect place to start filling in the above objections by supplying evidence (#5) in the form of testimonials.

Every time we wonder if something could be added or strengthened, we're highlighting possible objections. When you're reading copy, keep objections in mind at all times (it helps to have a sceptical mind - listen out for your inner voice - anything that triggers a negative emotion tells you something is off).

So let's go with #7 ("What are people saying about it?") and at the same time complete #3 ("Who was involved?") and #5 ("What evidence is there?"). Here are the next couple of paragraphs:

"Mike and Dorris are not alone though. Alan from Linton reported an income of $7,350 during his first quarter's use. You can see his verified testimonial here [insert link] along with hundreds of others who have had the same DIY home wind farm newly installed.

In fact the award-winning company who manufacture, supply, and fit this cutting-edge home energy solution have been doing it for decades, but up till now, it's only been available for commercial customers.

That's why the ABC DIY Home Wind Farm technology has a 30 year proven record of reliance, backed by a 10 year guarantee. If anything should go wrong, it will be repaired or replaced at no cost within 48 hours."

Item #8 in our blueprint ("Could it happen again?") is not relevant, and the last item (#9 "Why does it matter?") has been covered already. However, we could enhance that too. Here's the next paragraph:

"With global warming now a reality, producing renewable energy is at the top of the agenda, so you'll not only no longer be reliant on the giant utility companies and their ever increasing bills, you'll be helping to save the planet too."

With that we're done with the body copy of our ad. We've added a bunch more features and given each one at least one benefit.

The final point in our list (#10 How can I find out more?) is the call to action. The part where we tell our prospects how they can take advantage of this breakthrough technology. Here's the final paragraph:

"To find out how you can own and install the complete system and take advantage of this breakthrough technology, call ABC Energy direct on [insert phone number]"

Below is the advert so far after another couple of minor edits. A good exercise to do with any ads you come across is to read the copy from top to bottom and compile a list of all the features and benefits you find.

I'll do that now with this ad, but before you look at my list, read the ad in full next, then create your own list from it. What you're doing is reverse engineering the ad. Start doing this regularly and you'll train your brain to recognise good structure and pick up ideas about features, benefits, and advantages:

========START========
Couple Take On Energy Companies And Win

When Mike and Doris Taylor got their highest ever energy bill earlier this year, they decided they'd had enough of paying exorbitant costs to utility companies, and started looking for alternative energy sources - ideally, ones they could run themselves.

After a quick search on Google, they discovered two things. The first was that they could own their own energy producing equipment without stumping up a small fortune, the second was that they could profit from it by plugging it into the national grid.

What was it Mike and Doris stumbled on? A DIY home wind farm. Within two weeks it was built and up and running supplying more than enough electricity to heat their house with the built-in storage batteries allowing a 24/7 supply regardless of how much wind there was on any particular day. And with the excess electricity going direct to the national grid they were on to a nice little earner too.

Mike and Dorris are not alone though. Alan from Linton reported an income of $7,350 during his first quarter's use. You can see his verified testimonial here [link] along with hundreds of others who have had the same DIY home wind farm newly installed.

In fact the award-winning company who manufacture, supply, and fit this cutting-edge home energy solution (ABC Energy) have been doing it for decades, but up till now, it's only been available for commercial customers.

That's why the ABC DIY Home Wind Farm technology has a 30 year proven record of reliability, backed by a 10 year guarantee. If anything should go wrong, it will be repaired or replaced at no cost within 48 hours.

With global warming now a reality, producing renewable energy is at the top of the agenda, so you'll not only no longer be reliant on the giant utility companies and their

119

ever increasing bills, you'll be helping to save the planet too.

To find out how you can own and install the complete system and take advantage of this breakthrough technology, call ABC Energy direct on [insert phone number]
========END=======

Here's the list of features and benefits from the complete ad. Starting from the top:

1. "own energy producing equipment without stumping up a small fortune" - the feature is you can own it, the benefit is it costs less than you might expect (if you value money, this is an important benefit)
2. "profit from it by plugging it into the national grid" - the feature is you can plug it into the national grid, the benefit is you can profit from it
3. "Within two weeks it was built" - the feature is it takes two weeks to build, no benefit mentioned (could we improve this?)
4. "supplying more than enough electricity" - the feature is it supplies electricity, no benefit mentioned (could we improve this?)
5. "heat their house " - the feature is it heats houses, no benefit mentioned (could we improve this?)
6. "built-in storage batteries " - the feature is it has storage batteries, no benefit mentioned (could we improve this?)
7. "24/7 supply" - the feature is it is available 24/7, no benefit mentioned (could we improve this?)
8. "direct to the national grid they were on to a nice little earner" - the feature is it supplies the national

grid, the benefit is extra income (a slight twist on benefit #2 that identified profit as the benefit)

9. "home energy solution" - the feature is it can be run from home, no benefit mentioned (could we improve this?)

10. "10 year guarantee" - the feature is it has a 10 year guarantee, no benefit mentioned (could we improve this?)

11. "repaired or replaced at no cost within 48 hours" - the feature is it will be repaired or replaced within 48 hours if it goes wrong, the benefit is there's no cost

12. "you'll no longer be reliant on the giant utility companies" - the feature is it's independent, the benefit is you won't need to rely on other services

13. "you'll be helping to save the planet" - the feature is it helps save the planet, the benefit is you'll feel better about owning it

14. "call ABC Energy direct" - the feature is: it's available direct from the manufacturer, no benefit mentioned (could we improve this?)

As I mentioned earlier, some benefits are implied depending on the awareness of the prospect. For example, if someone values a guarantee (#10 in our list), then the guarantee alone is of benefit to them, but if they don't yet value guarantees, then the benefits need to be explained along with how that guarantee is going to be met (proof).

How can we improve some of those features that don't yet have clear benefits? If we look at feature #5 ("heat their house"), we could add something like "and never feel cold again in winter", or "for a fraction of the price others are paying."

For #6 ("built-in storage batteries") the benefit is obvious to most people, but spelling it out wouldn't hurt, e.g., "so your electricity supply is never interrupted even if there's no wind", but we could go further by showing why being subservient to a utility company is worse than most people think, e.g., "and what's more, if there's a national or local power cut, it won't affect you at all, so you can relax, and watch TV with a nice cup of tea when everyone else in the neighbourhood is searching around in the dark for a torch or a candle and matches."

The exact same benefits can be applied to #7 as well, but if you look at #9, it's not quite so simple. This is because "home energy solution" is so broad. We use simple descriptions like this in copy to make it clear what the thing being sold is (it answers the question "what is a home wind farm?" should a reader still be unclear).

With a little thought you can add many more benefits to every feature, but this needs to be done with care or you'll start to overwhelm the prospect and they may get distracted, or worse, start to ask for more proof, and eventually stop reading in disbelief if we don't supply it (the "too good to be true" syndrome).

The other pitfall is boring them with benefits or being condescending by pointing out the obvious: "having four wheels means your car is more stable on the road making you feel safer when driving." Duh!

Benefits without features

One other thing worth mentioning is that some ads go overboard with benefits and forget to mention features. This is also done on purpose with what is called 'blind copy' (especially prevalent in the internet marketing industry).

If I list a whole bunch of benefits without referring to the basics (such as "what is it?") I will certainly increase curiosity, but I run the risk of false selling or click baiting - which often results in bad reactions from authorities with the power to not just remove adverts, but fine us or worse.

You'll find this kind of advertising in most 'make money from home' or 'get rich quick' scams. In fact one sign of those schemes is when the advertiser states in their copy that it is "NOT a get rich quick scheme", or that it's "NOT for people who want to get rich quick" (villains always deny the very thing they're doing).

Blind copy

Let's look at a typical example (this one is entirely fictitious):

========START========
How To Earn 6 Figures In 6 Days Without Lifting A Finger

Ever wondered how some people end up rich without having to do any work? Read on...

If I could show you how to earn 6 figures in 6 days that would allow you to finally fire your boss, look after yourself and your family for the rest of your lives, and buy the house of your dreams for cash, what would that be worth to you?

Well I can, and whilst I realise that seems unbelievable, by the time you've finished reading this 'nothing left out' report, you'll know exactly what to do.

========END=======

The above 'report' can go on for page after page revealing almost nothing about what it is it's actually selling. It doesn't need to because that's not its point. It's a blind sale (because it uses blind copy), so the truth will never be revealed (until the prospect follows the call to action and pays the money to find out).

Adverts like the above fail on every count when it comes to legitimate selling in every country where such laws exist (which is practically all of them).

Here's the first item from the Federal Trade Commission's Advertising and Marketing Basics rules (the FTC is the USA's watchdog with teeth when it comes to false claims in selling):

"Under the law, claims in advertisements must be truthful, cannot be deceptive or unfair, and must be evidence-based. For some specialized products or services, additional rules may apply."

You'd think that if you could provide the evidence to support a blind copy ad, then all would be good, but you'd be wrong. If there's any sign of deception at all (and blind copy is the acme of that), the FTC will be all over it (and even if you prove your case, you may well be locked out of doing business for some considerable time - not to mention the considerable legal and other costs incurred from defending such an action).

To summarise, features without benefits is fine but won't get many sales. Benefits without features almost always breaks the law, so always stick to features and benefits (advantages matter too - see FAB in the glossary, but remember they're benefits too, they just happen to be benefits that no one else has exploited yet).

Going back to our wind farm ad again, the last item without an obvious benefit is #14: "call ABC Energy direct." That brings us to the next stage in building an ad (short or long copy).

Call to action

In our ad, our call to action consists of 4 words, two of which are the name of the company ("call ABC Energy direct"). A call to action is exactly what it sounds like. We are asking the reader to do something.

What that something is varies depending on the purpose of the ad. If the purpose is to sell something, then the most likely message will be "Buy Now" with a means to do that (e.g., click a button to take us to a shopping cart).

If the purpose is to get someone to sign up to something, it's also a call to action. In fact, anything that asks someone to do something is a call to action. It's important to understand what seems obvious to most because the one thing that people overlook in advertising (especially online) is too many DIFFERENT calls to action in a single ad.

What I mean by that is an ad where we give people more than a single choice to buy the thing the ad is selling. For example: "get this today from a wide range of stockists, direct from our own website, or call our helpline for more information."

You might think this is fine, but the problem is, we're giving our prospects a very real chance of not doing anything at all because they're not quite sure what to do ("should I look for a stockist near me? Or maybe I should call the company and find out their prices? In which case, I wonder if there's any discount available?" and so on).

When we force our prospects to make a decision (other than whether they're going to buy or not) we put obstacles in their way (even though we think we're being helpful). It can also come across as desperate, which hurts conversion rates - see the subsection on Negotiation in chapter 11 for more on desperation and how this adversely affects sales.

This is not the same as multiple calls to the same action in a single ad: e.g., a buy now button placed throughout the copy.

Care needs to be taken with this approach though, since it can result in someone seeing the price before they have been sold on the value (that doesn't automatically stop a sale, it just raises the bar before you have a chance of explaining why the bar may be so high in the first place).

This, like all things in advertising, also varies by awareness. If someone's looking to buy a Rolex watch, they already know it's going to cost some serious money, so discovering that the latest model is £99,999 before being told why it's worth every cent will not surprise them (and may even be a good thing from the point of view of removing prospects that would never dream of spending that much).

There's another way of adding multiple calls to action to the same end, and that's by varying the text. This is often used in email marketing (see Appendix E - Email marketing). It works when the result of carrying out the call to action (e.g., what happens when someone clicks a link) is the same thing.

Take a look at this:

========EMAIL EXAMPLE START========
Dear Subscriber,

Today we celebrate our centenary, and to thank you for being part of that journey, we'd like to invite you to an exclusive event [insert link to the words 'exclusive event' - this is called an anchor or 'anchor text' in HTML terminology].

Obviously, no one wants to waste their time, so we're including a valuable bonus [insert same link as above to the 'valuable bonus' anchor text] - you'll get to see what that is when you attend (suffice to say we know you'll love it). [insert same link on 'attend'].

The event takes place on xx/xx/xxxx at 9pm ET and is limited to 100 seats (the platform limit), so book your place [insert same link to 'book your place'] now to ensure you get in.

See you in a couple of days.

Yours xxxxxx
========EMAIL EXAMPLE END========

Multiple calls to action, everyone a little different, yet they all point to the same place and the reader will not mind, because every link delivered on the promise.

You can do the same with any type copy by using segmented calls to action. For example, there's nothing wrong with adding something like "Want to know more about XYZ?" earlier in your copy if it helps to answer an objection and leads to another landing page that continues the journey you want the reader to take.

This is an excellent way of segmenting readers with different awareness levels who have just landed on a page they might otherwise reject.

What I mean by that is, for example, where a reader has landed on a page aimed at an aware audience, but who, whilst still being interested, has not heard of the product being sold. In this case, adding something like "New to XYZ? Find out more" will segment them off to a less aware landing page that takes up the story.

Also, adding a "Ready to buy now? Click here" button as a CTA anywhere in your copy will help those who are revisiting the page, or really are ready to buy now. It does run the risk of those more interested in the cost, clicking and then rejecting the offer because they have not yet been sold on its value.

You can get very creative with CTAs as you can see. The critical thing is to know why you are doing it (i.e., don't add CTAs like this everywhere just because you can or it seems like a good idea, do it for the right reason - which means being very aware of the type of audience you're attracting and their reactions and objections).

Guarantees

A guarantee is there to handle further objections. If your copy fails to convince the prospect that what you're selling is not only fit for purpose, but fit for THEIR purpose (and that they need to buy it right now), then a guarantee can get them closer to the tipping point. Whilst that may be true, it's not the best reason to include one.

What a guarantee should do is increase confidence to buy, not confidence that if the product is crap, they can get their money back. So should you include one at all, and if so, how would you do that? Let's dig deeper.

It has been said many times that if you have a guarantee, flaunt it, and whilst this sounds like good advice, I have never found it to move the needle in any meaningful way unless the guarantee is outrageous and/or the offer is too good to be true.

In other words, it's used heavily in the internet marketing industry to move products that would otherwise not sell at all, but rarely works out there in the real world of brick and mortar products because most of us are not duped by dubious claims.

Also, we've become used to guarantees, and most of us only respect guarantees from well established businesses anyway. Guarantees from anyone else we tend to treat with a pinch of salt (e.g., "I know it says it has a 10 year guarantee, but will the company still be around in 10 years?" or "probably not worth the paper it's written on").

Because we've been subjected to a lifetime of being upsold guarantees from retailers selling electronic equipment and white goods (via insurance), we've come to learn that if something has a manufacturer's twelve month guarantee, it's probably good for three years anyway, so why waste any money on it when we can just buy a new one if it goes wrong, because it might well last ten years.

Having said that, guarantees are still an important good faith indicator to people (you just don't need to go overboard selling it - assuming the product or service you're promoting does what it claims to do).

One thing to watch out for are so-called 'lifetime' guarantees. The implication is that it will last YOUR lifetime, but this is rarely stated. It's just the way we, as prospects, interpret it. The FTC and many other compliance authorities (including credit card companies) have indicated they are either investigating these claims, and in many cases, have outlawed them.

In the UK, claims like this could breach the Consumer Rights Act 2015 or the UK Code of Non-broadcast Advertising and Direct and Promotional Marketing (known as the CAP Code).

If a client asks you to write such things, you may be wise in explaining there can be legal consequences in using terms that cannot be substantiated (you might also be wise in obtaining written proof of your conversation in case it ever comes back to you - always seek legal advice when in doubt).

Bonuses

Bonuses are the bread and butter of the internet marketing industry (IM) - it's rare to see any IM launch that doesn't include a whole bunch of bonuses - especially from affiliates trying to get to the top of a JV launch campaign - see Joint venture (JV) in the glossary.

There are two types of copywriter - actually there are many, but there is a clear distinction between those who write for the internet marketing industry and those who write for the rest of the business world.

The internet marketing industry revolves around information products (including eBooks, courses, membership sites, and more recently, software). It also revolves around affiliate marketing (if you think of the internet marketing industry as the affiliate marketing industry, you'll have it about right).

Those at the top know each other and promote each other's products and launches. It's pretty much quid pro quo, except by joining forces they're creating a larger market, and by implication a larger pot of money to spread around.

The goal is to sell as much product as possible regardless of the consequences. The carrot is often the same as well for anyone buying into most of these products, and that is, by buying into them you too can promote them and join as an affiliate (and later perhaps, sign up as a joint venture partner).

In order to fulfil that goal, every angle has been tried and tested in the IM industry from outrageous guarantees to offers with literally hundreds of bonuses. People have also offered 200% (and more) affiliate commissions (which means for every dollar an affiliate brings into the business, the affiliate gets two dollars back).

Economically, that sounds like lunacy, but these high commission rates are only offered on what is called the "front end" of the system (the lowest price point in a long funnel of upsells, downsells, cross sells, repeat sales, and subscriptions - also known as continuity schemes).

The rest of a typical internet marketing sales funnel is called the "back end", and is where the real money is made. The most common phrase you'll find for this is the notion of "not leaving money on the table." The idea is that once the prospect has their wallet out and bought something, it's easier to sell them on other things whilst they're still hot.

The funnel system has now evolved into a deeply engineered art form with some funnels being so long and complicated, you need extensive software to keep track of it all.

The crazy thing about the IM industry is that the promises are so outrageous (e.g., "Earn 8 figures in 8 weeks doing this one thing") that it becomes highly addictive to those on both sides of the equation - the buyers and the sellers, and as a result, you'll see product launch after product launch, day after day, month after month, and year after year.

Many of these products have disappeared nearly as fast as they came, and for those on the darker side of the industry, they are nothing more than multi-level marketing schemes anyway.

This is why you never see these types of deals in mainstream business. They can't get away with it - as soon as the business becomes big enough, it attracts the attention of the authorities.

It is for this reason alone that you should focus on professional copywriting for real businesses and not the IM industry if you want a long-term satisfying and ethical career.

That's not to say that every IM business is like this. There are plenty of ethical IM businesses out there, but where you see joint ventures and tons of promotional material aimed at affiliates, take a great deal of care.

So how does the normal business world operate when it comes to bonuses? It's quite limited, but the most common are: Buy one, get one free (known as BOGOF in the retail trade) and variations of this (e.g., buy three get one free and buy one get a second half price).

Normal businesses will also add relevant extra items to increase the perceived value of the main offer (very common in car advertisements - e.g., "Now includes xyz as standard").

Other incentives and persuaders

It's not just bonuses that can be used to increase sales by adding extra perceived value to offers. The most common is to limit an offer by time or quantity. The value this adds is scarcity, speaking of which, you'll find it useful to memorise my simple acronym called SURE to remind you of the four key conversion tools of any CTA.

These are:

S: Scarcity
U: Urgency
R: Rarity
E: Exclusivity

Although they may sound similar, each has their place.

Scarcity: Something that is scarce means it's hard to find (it doesn't necessarily mean there's a limit on total numbers even though dictionaries often tie it in with rarity).

Urgency: Something that is urgent lets us know it's not going to be around forever (or it may cost a lot more, or be unobtainable if we don't act fast).

Rarity: Means there are limited numbers. It's more specific than scarcity.

Exclusivity. This implies rareness and scarcity but is entirely different when it comes to selling luxury goods. For example, not everyone can afford a Ferrari, but equally, not everyone is allowed to buy a Ferrari. Ferrari often create exclusive cars that only certain people on their internal customer and prospect list are allowed to buy. This keeps up the perceived exclusiveness of being a Ferrari owner (and therefore the price of such cars).

Of these, by far the most important when it comes to pushing sales fast are time limited offers. That's what urgency is all about. Every time we see a "SALE" poster or ad, we're put on a timing alert.

We know it will end soon even though many companies (particularly in the household furnishing market) seem to be perpetually having a sale. It has a similar effect to the word NEW in terms of getting our attention.

The sale must end at some point though - or the urgency to buy is lost. Sales are usually done to promote specific items that are sold at a loss in order to attract more customers. The idea is that they are then more likely to buy other products that are not discounted to make up for the loss.

The first three of our persuaders - scarcity, urgency, and rarity, are also synonymous with FOMO (the fear of missing out - see Appendix F - Fear), so can be used effectively in tandem, whereas the fourth persuader (exclusivity) has more to do with desire, status, and ownership.

Shopping cart

The final part of any online call to action that involves a sale is the shopping cart, and our copy matters just as much there as it does anywhere else. Keep this in mind when talking with a prospect - a good copywriter should be responsible for all the words in a sales piece, not just the headline and body copy (it adds extra value to your proposition not just in terms of how much you get paid, but how knowledgeable and caring you are of the whole process).

According to statistics from major vendors and ecommerce merchants, many sales are still lost at the shopping cart stage. This is partly through bad shopping cart software, but also due to not continuing the sense of value and caring the customer feels at the point where they're about to part with their money.

That means care needs to be taken to ensure the shopping cart experience involves the least possible resistance technology wise, and also that the words used in the shopping cart are aligned with the words used in the advert that got them there in the first place.

For example, if you included a strong guarantee in your copy, repeat it at the shopping cart stage. If you included bonuses or other persuaders and value-adds, then make sure they're also repeated so the customer is reassured that this is the deal for them.

Bump offers

Some shopping carts allow bump offers. These are another form of upsell in that they allow the customer to add something extra to their order simply by ticking a box. These can greatly increase the order value and work well if the offer is directly related to what's being bought.

A good example is a book purchase where the bump offer is to add the audible version of the book to the order. In other words, the product is perfectly good as it is, but, as in this example, there's another way to consume it that the buyer may find valuable.

Sale stoppers

A big problem with offers, especially in terms of need, is where a prospect finds an offer both desirable and affordable, but has no need of it right now. To overcome that, the copy needs to switch to a 'just in case' angle.

That is how most insurance is sold, but it can apply to anything and it's useful to know how to word offers like this to open a market wider than just those who are currently in need of such a product.

Let's take an example. A man, aged around 50, once had a boyhood dream of playing the guitar. In particular, he wanted to be Mark Knopfler (from Dire Straits). The desire is there, but it has long been ignored.

Then one day he stumbles across Dire Straits' Money for Nothing track on YouTube, listens to it nostalgically, and is then remarketed to by a company offering an online guitar course.

He doesn't need the course (and is certainly not in the market right now for buying one), but the advertiser is aware of this, and ensures that the landing page the ad points to is geared up for just such a prospect.

There are an unlimited number of angles the ad could take, so here's an example of one of them. The big idea is to paint a future where the audience who watch the ad have grown too old to even pick up a guitar and they now regret they didn't take advantage of the one thing they'd always wanted to do but never got around to.

From an image point of view, we could have an octogenarian sitting in an armchair in an old people's home watching a video of Mark Knopfler. He's playing along with tiny movements of his arthritic hands as though he had an air guitar.

The look on his face is pure pleasure laced with just a hint of regret. As the music plays, he imagines he's back in his youth picking up a guitar to learn how to play.

At this point, the voiceover and caption says something like "It's never too late to learn guitar..."

With that in mind, it's time to write the rest of the script. Let's start as usual with the feature list. If the prospect is made aware a product exists (in this example, our guitar course), then all we need to do is state the problem this product fixes.

As you can see from the ad outline, we're creating the problem for them. We're also reminding them that if they ever want to fulfil their dream, time is running out.

So our feature list needs to identify the sort of features that play on whatever problems we want to highlight that our audience will pay attention to. For example: "play your first song in less than 5 minutes." Think about what problems that feature implies in relation to our prospect, and then think about how those problems are solved. It might be something like "easy to learn whether you're eight or eighty."

What we've done is identify a benefit from that feature. It's easy to identify benefits this way when you put yourself in your prospect's shoes and figure out the problem they NEED to have if they're going to buy your product.

Here's another feature: "includes over the shoulder chord progressions for all your favourite songs." This is described as a feature and not a benefit because there's no connecting words in it, such as: "so that you can...."

Let's break it down into benefits. But first, you may have noticed there are multiple features in that one sentence:

1. Over the shoulder
2. Chord progressions
3. Favourite songs

What is good about 'over the shoulder' tutorials? We can see HOW it's done (prefer showing over telling). What's good about chord progressions? We'll have no idea how to play the piece unless we know the chords. And what's great about having chord progressions to our 'favourite songs'? We'll be able to play the one or more songs that our dreams were made of in our youth.

We'll go with those couple of feature examples for the body copy of our script. Obviously, the longer the video, the more script we'll need, but because the medium is video, we probably don't need that many words.

With that in mind, here's a simple first draft:

========START========
Scene 1: It's never too late to learn guitar...
Scene 2: Whether your eight or eighty...
Scene 3: But with your favourite songs included...
Scene 4: And every chord progression made simple...
Scene 5: You might just want to start playing right now...
========END========

If we wanted to outline more features relevant to our big idea (that it's never too late to learn guitar) we could increase the video to any length we wanted.

As long as we keep it aligned with our prospect's problem (including highlighting that there is one) and ensure that every word builds desire and handles any objections along the way, it makes it possible to increase our market share from just those who are ready to buy now, to a far wider audience (e.g., those who once had an interest in learning the guitar but have not yet got nostalgic about it).

As you can see, ads like this are perfect for video since the prospect has already been watching videos and the advertiser knows that would be the best medium to use to build desire.

This is another example of the sort of work copywriters do or can advertise themselves as doing in order to differentiate themselves in the market. Also, anyone positioning themselves this way will be seen as a specialist, and as we know, specialists always command higher fees.

Let's take another example. The prospect for this is a 30 year old mother of two young children who sometimes struggles to meet the demands she has placed on herself because of her deep sense of responsibility.

She has a problem (which often results in stress) but she's not sure what that problem is or how to resolve it (she just knows she gets stressed sometimes). Our job is to persuade her that she needs yoga to help her cope so she'll buy into an online yoga class we're selling.

The problem we have is that whilst she will have heard of yoga, it's unlikely to be front of mind right now - or even something that she'd consider as a possible solution.

This is slightly different from the 'just in case' scenario, but the concept is the same in that we're trying to sell something to someone who has not considered what we're selling as a solution (or even admits she has a problem).

This is the toughest of all markets to convince, but imagine what would happen if we could?

The good news is we KNOW she has a problem, and we KNOW that problem is stress, so now we need to convince her of this, and that there's only one solution that will end it forever.

Here are the features of our yoga class:
1. It's online
2. It's for beginners
3. It's a low-cost subscription
4. It relaxes the mind and body
5. It increases flexibility in the body
6. It can be practiced at home
7. It's personalised for each member
8. Each member has access to a personal trainer

I created this list by looking at the competition. If you want a winning product (or you've been asked to promote a client's product) check out the competition by looking at every paid ad you see.

That way you'll discover what matters (assuming the paid ads are converting) and what, if anything, is missing from your offer (so you can discuss it with your client in the hope that they'll improve their yoga class - to make it easier for you to write the copy that sells it).

Now we have to decide which of these features match up with our target audience's likely needs. For me, that would be features 1 to 6, with 7 and 8 being optional (although item 3 depends on other demographics, so may be irrelevant).

We'll identify the relevant benefits in a minute, but first we need to find a big idea. At the time of writing, the whole world is in a state of partial lockdown due to the COVID-19 pandemic, so we can assume many people are stuck at home with no notion of how long it may last.

Therefore item 6 (practice at home) is important. There's also an implication that when we're stuck at home, we may feel more isolated, so perhaps the idea of having a friend on call 24/7 to help us may work.

Also, because we know our target is more towards the 'unaware' end of the awareness spectrum, we need some kind of headline that both calls the prospect out, and either (1) suggests there's a problem, or (2) implies that life can be improved.

Let's explore the first option:

(1) "Stuck at home with kids and feeling stressed?"

And now the second (which extends the first):

(2) "Stuck at home with kids and feeling stressed? Read this."

The "Read this" lets the prospect know there's a solution coming (and is, in effect, also a call to action - telling the reader to continue reading).

We could get more explicit:

"Mother, stuck at home with two kids, feeling stressed, tries this."

This last headline changes the point of view (POV) from first person to third person. By doing so, it removes any negativity about being told what to do, and instead uses a third person example implying and suggesting that "others are doing this - therefore maybe you should too."

But it also sounds rather sucky (i.e., like the many click bait ads we see online - e.g., "Mother of two opens her front door and is shocked by what she discovers on her doormat" - don't do this unless the purpose of the ad is to increase click-through rates and you have no problem with the ethics of doing it).

Let's try another angle - the 24/7 friend approach mentioned earlier:

"How to cope with stress. Meet your new friend for life."

I've removed the 'home', 'mother', and 'kids' elements from the earlier headlines to make it simpler and also made 'how to cope' the subject of the headline, and 'stress' the object (i.e., the problem) that needs fixing. This is followed by an implication that something amazing is about to be revealed ('new friend for life').

If our prospect happens to be feeling stressed when this ad pops up on, say, her news feed, she might well click it. But if she's feeling happy or in some other mood, it will fly right past and be ignored (which is a good thing, as this ad is not for someone who's feeling fine - we are not trying to attract those people with an ad with a headline like this, so we don't want to waste money every time one of them clicks it).

This brings up an important point for headlines. Whilst it makes sense to call out our target audience, it makes no sense at all if our target audience is not interested in this particular offer at this time UNLESS we can engage them and change their mood in the body copy of our landing page.

In the case of our example, there are millions of mums with two kids who feel stress from time to time, but we know that only those who are feeling stressed at this time will be interested in finding (and possibly buying) a solution.

This is why, when we think in terms of 'just in case', we can change our copy to attract, engage, and maybe convert all mothers, no matter what they're feeling right now to buy our product.

"Great news for all young mothers. Meet your new friend for life."

We're calling out our target audience again ('news' is the subject of this headline, and 'young mothers' is the object). We've added our big idea 'friend for life' and used intrigue as our angle (the intrigue is "what great news?" and "who is this new friend?" - that's what we want our prospects to subconsciously start thinking about).

We've also implied this is about their future (with the words 'for life'). We've made the headline positive instead of negative by removing words like 'stress'. But more importantly, we're using futurescaping to give our audience hope.

Futurescaping shows people what their future may be like and implies there's a way to make it better. Because this builds hope, we can easily return them to their current situation to emphasize the difference between where they are now and where they could be.

Let's do that in the subheadline:
"For all those currently stuck at home who get stressed from time to time."

This gets straight to the point. We've suggested a rosy future with a new friend, then pointed out that whilst life may not be so rosy right now, a solution is about to be revealed.

We've also highlighted feature 6 (use at home) and implied a benefit (if you're stuck at home, this solution will give you a friend - and maybe you won't feel so lonely or stressed any more).

Up to this point, our landing page consists of blind copy (we haven't explained what it is or what it does). Here's the lede:

===START===
Julie, 29, and mother of two toddlers, loves motherhood as much as anyone, but when Emmy, her youngest, became desperately ill, it affected her more deeply than she at first realised.

She started eating more, she slept less, and it began to affect her close family relationships too.

But it was her partner, Jim who sounded the alarm. He'd noticed the signs and knew he had to find a way to help.
===END===

We've implemented the classic "it's not your fault" psychological tactic with this lede. We've also introduced an association by talking about Julie's partner, and the big idea is there with the idea of a friend (although we've not yet introduced who that 'friend' really is - yoga).

Let's continue into the body copy:

===START===
Jim had heard from a friend that they'd changed not just their life, but their relationships and fitness too with a simple set of exercises used the world over. And what's more, it was something recommended by all health experts for reducing stress.

It turns out there were classes everywhere including online, and that anyone could do these in their own home in privacy. But how do you let someone know there's a solution without sounding like a jerk?
===END===

We still don't know what this thing is, but we now know what it does, that it does it well, that it's used the world over, and that you can access it anywhere. That's a whole bunch of features, benefits, and objections handled in just a few sentences.

At this point, the prospect may well have scanned down the ad looking for what this wondrous solution is, but that's fine. We've hooked them into the story, and now it's a matter of keeping them there.

We've included features 1, 4, 5, and 6 from our list too (it's online, it relaxes the mind and body, it increases flexibility in the body, it can be practiced at home). And we've opened a loop - "how do you explain this without sounding like a jerk?"

The idea is that we handle a possible objection by showing that her partner cares enough to respect Julie's sense of pride and finding her own solution - after all, she's not sure she needs a solution yet, so having one forced down her throat is not going to work.

Let's continue with the body copy:

===START===
Jim did this in one simple step. He signed up to an online yoga class. He told Julie he sometimes felt a little depressed, and that he'd heard that yoga would improve his body and mind so he'd not only feel better, he could help more around the house."
===END===

The idea is to reassure our prospect that not only would this solution help her too, it was something other people did to improve their lives.

We could continue in this way for some time by adding more features and benefits using the show don't tell method (and handling objections in the process), but let's cut to the close and the call to action:

===START===
The online class Jim found is called Yoga Club. It's available 24/7, includes a personal trainer, individually tailored lessons, and is aimed firmly at those new to yoga. Julie signed up as soon as she saw the changes yoga was having on Jim, and because Yoga Club has a family option, she's getting her girls involved too. If you want to

find out more, visit our website: club.yoga and get started for less than the cost of a cup of coffee a day.
===END===

The above uses the problem, agitate, solution (PAS) framework to weave its way from beginning to end. This framework starts by exposing a problem, then agitating that problem to increase the internal pressure on the prospect to find a solution, and with that done, ends by explaining the solution (followed by a call to action to buy it).

Like all frameworks, they're useful to know, but none are magic bullets. The difference between any campaign working or failing depends on far more than a framework, blueprint, or template.

Just think of them as guides you can turn to if you get stuck on how to structure a story or any other piece of copy. Another popular guide you'll probably have heard of is AIDA. You'll find details on that (and PAS) in the glossary.

There's one more thing worth reminding you of at this point. Your first draft of any copy is rarely, if ever, right. And even if it does seem OK when you've just written it, I can guarantee that if you leave it for a day or two then come back and reread it, you will find snags (and perhaps even wonder why you thought it was good at all).

This point can never be stressed enough no matter how good a copywriter you are. Never accept your first draft (and never show a first draft to a client). This where editing comes in, and that's where we're headed next.

10 Editing

Before we get into editing and just how important that is, we need to take a close look at our mindset. If you write and edit with the wrong mindset, you'll end up with poor copy. It's not so much a Zen thing, it's really just common sense. Every copywriter (and writer) I've ever met has made the same mistake at the start of their careers of failing to edit some or all of their first drafts.

There's a brilliant scene in the film Toy Story 2 where Geri "The Cleaner" is asked to tidy up Woody and is asked how long it will take. His reply is: "You can't rush art", and that's the best advice you can ever get when it comes to copy.

Most copy fails to do what its writer wants it to do. Add to that, the sheer volume of failed copy not just out there already, but growing exponentially every day.

Unless your copy hits the right spot for the right audience with the right offer (i.e., a unique solution only available now) then it will fail just like every other piece of badly written or badly targeted copy.

And on that note, think about this:

Any piece of copy, no matter how well written IS badly written from the wrong audience's point of view. How do I know? Because it doesn't convert. That's all that matters. Copy either converts (in terms of sales) or doesn't. Any copy that doesn't is bad copy because it's not doing what it was intended to do.

There's a simple phrase you need to keep at the forefront of your mind every time you write a piece of copy, and it's this: "don't be precious." I refer you back to chapter 4 and the subsection 'Precious' in case you've forgotten why it matters.

But my point is, 'not being precious' applies just as much to editing as it does to writing copy in the first place.

If you're reading a piece of copy and something doesn't quite work, you have a choice: edit it to make it work, or delete it entirely. Often the latter is the best thing to do, but I know from long experience how hard it is to delete what we first thought was something brilliant and unique.

It goes further than that though. You'll find that if you delete a sentence or paragraph, a rewrite of what preceded and what follows is almost always required, and as soon as you realise that, there's a good chance you'll waste time trying to keep the original offending piece of copy in place by editing it instead of deleting it.

If that happens, remember what I said earlier - most copy fails, and it fails because it's not good enough (wrong message, wrong audience, or plain bad copy).

Once you know something is 'badly written' (for whatever reason regardless of whether it might win the Pulitzer Prize), you'll become less precious about your writing. That's the state you need to be in.

Your mind is an incredible, creative, and infinite source of words, invention, and imagination. The more you write, the more it improves (I had no idea how true this was until I started writing on purpose every day - even if it was just trivial stuff in my daily journal).

Once you realise you can happily chuck away everything because you will always be improving, you'll lose your precious writing pride (which we all start with), and from that point on, you'll become unstoppable.

So with all that in mind, let's talk about editing.

Your first drafts

The problem with editing our own work is our memories. The sooner we start editing what we've written, the worse the editing becomes. This is because we're still in the story so to speak - we're still too close to what we've just written to edit it objectively.

NOTE: in case that depresses you, here's a glimmer of hope, the more you edit your work following the instructions presented in this chapter, the better you will get at it. As a result, the gap between writing and editing diminishes, and as that gap gets smaller, your first drafts will also start improving. In the end, everything speeds up. You just need to keep writing copy and edit it consistently.

Another way to understand the memory issue is to read a piece of copy you've never seen before (it doesn't matter whose copy you read). You're getting an instant first impression. And along with that impression, you will start feeling many different emotions.

Each emotion you feel tells you everything you need to know about that copy. Has it moved you in some way? Were you bored with the first sentence? Did some parts leave you confused? Did any typos stop you reading instantly? Did anything else interrupt the flow? Did you understand what it was about? And a whole load more.

Those are the questions you need to be asking of your own copy, but if you still hold much of what you wrote in memory, then your objectivity will be compromised. In other words, the difference between a good and bad editor (or editing session) is down to how objective the editor and the editing is. We'll get into how that's done shortly. Meanwhile, back to first drafts and how to approach them.

People are different when it comes to first drafts. Some prefer to write slowly and edit out obvious mistakes as they go along (I fall into that camp). Others will write a first draft without editing a single word until it's done (this is the most common advice from other gurus by the way).

Which of these you choose depends on you and your ability to forget what you've just written. If you can learn to forget what you wrote ten minutes after writing it, then you're good whichever method you choose. If not, you'll need longer and may be better off adopting the zero edit approach until you've finished your first draft.

Of all the things that stop us in our stride when both writing and editing, it's making writing tougher than it needs to be (think about the idea of preciousness we just talked about, and you'll see why not being precious also matters when it comes to writing first drafts).

The good news is that this is a simple choice. If you can't stop yourself editing out errors as you go along, then don't fight it. On the other hand, if you love writing non-stop without editing, then that is your first draft style (this is just like being left-handed or right-handed - don't let others force you into doing something that feels awkward to you).

But equally, I encourage you to experiment. If you've never tried writing a draft without editing, give it a go. Maybe you'll find that easier. One way to do that is called speed writing. Set yourself a timer of say, ten minutes, and write non-stop until the timer ends.

It doesn't matter what you write during those ten minutes (or what you write with - pen or computer). Writing complete gibberish is also fine, all that matters is you start and don't stop until the timer goes off (over time, your brain will kick in and you'll write something meaningful).

Whatever style you choose, this is still your first draft, and as such will ALWAYS require editing. As I alluded to earlier, no one ever wrote a single piece of work they didn't later want to revise (and that includes top authors, top composers, and artists - in fact every creative profession that exists).

Once you know this, you'll feel less precious about your work, and that will make you a stronger writer.

Fresh eyes

With your first draft done, I'd suggest you leave it for at least a day. How long entirely depends on your ability to forget what you wrote. This is also part of the mindset of being 'non-precious'.

The more non-precious you are, the faster you'll be able to put what you've written behind you, and the quicker you'll be able to go through the editing process.

We know we're ready to start editing copy when we feel as though we've not seen it before. This is really tough to do if you're new to copy but dead easy if you're an experienced journalist or writer of any kind. It takes practice to get to this state, but it will come.

I call it reading with Fresh Eyes. It's worth reiterating that the more you write and edit, the better you'll become at it.

The editing process

The goals of editing are many, but ultimately, we want something that is clear to EVERY potential prospect, is error free, and is so compelling to read, it cannot be put down until every last word has been read and consumed - the proof of which is a high conversion rate from the copy's call to action.

Before you ask what a high conversion rate is, all you need to know is that no other piece written to date with the same offer has converted more. For our first finished piece of copy, whatever rate it converts at becomes our initial highest converting rate (the control piece), and until we write something better, it will remain that way (this idea matters more than you may realise, and is discussed in the next chapter on prospecting).

There's another thing to know about the difference between a first draft and the final edited copy: the result will more often than not be shorter. If that's not the case, there are three reasons you may want to consider:

1. You left out important features or benefits.

2. Your copy wasn't clear enough.

3. Your editing was faulty.

Let's find out why that might be by going through the most important editing rules you need to keep in mind.

Emotions

When you read any copy, read it with an open mind. You need to learn to listen to your feelings and emotions as you go through it. The BEST way to do that when you're new to this is to READ IT ALOUD.

I cannot emphasise that enough. When you read any copy aloud, your ears physically hear it for the first time. It doesn't matter if you're self-conscious (this is often the case if you've not done this before), just try it.

This simple act will also do wonders for your confidence should you ever want (or need) to do any public speaking. Professional speakers (and actors) do this in front of a mirror so they can observe their expression and other body movements at the same time and ensure congruency between what they're saying and what they're displaying.

Reading your copy aloud will also help with your creativity. You'll start thinking of different ways to express your thoughts, which at first will lead to many edits, but that's great. As a copywriter, you'll find your real voice faster.

Whilst reading your copy aloud, listen and watch out for the following:

If you find yourself distracted, it means one of three things:

1. You have something else on your mind. Make sure you're prepared mentally to go into edit mode. I call this

"wearing the right hat." Imagine yourself as chief editor of the most prestigious publishing house on the planet. The expectation is that you never make mistakes and you're always 100% focused. Imagine also that the job comes complete with a hat labelled "Chief Editor." Every time you go into edit mode, imagine yourself putting on that hat so you BECOME that editor. Now find yourself a quiet place where you can't be distracted and get editing.

2. You're bored. This is a bad sign (but super important to notice). If you're bored by your own copy, I can guarantee that everyone else will be too. Remember this quote: "I make sure my writing is not boring by leaving out the boring parts."

3. You feel nothing as you're reading. The writer Robert Frost said "no tears in the writer no tears in the reader". If we're moved by our copy, it's a strong signal we're using emotional language, and that's a good sign.

As you're reading your first drafts, if you find yourself in any way confused, you are being told unequivocally that a rewrite of at least that sentence or section is necessary.

If you find yourself screwing up your eyes or any other facial features (except a broad smile), it's a sign something is not quite right. Figure out what it is (see chapter 12 Rules for guidance) and fix it.

If, by the end, you're not shouting "WOW - this is good" it's a sign that you need to improve the copy. Don't ignore this one.

Some people edit on the spot (i.e., as soon as their emotions tell them something's wrong, they change or delete the offending word/s or phrases immediately), others leave a mark of some sort in the copy and carry on reading until the end, then edit out all the mistakes.

I do the former - edit as I'm going along. If the edit is quick (e.g., a typo) I will edit and carry on. If it takes me more than a few seconds to correct - i.e., some thinking time is involved, I may well stop after that particular edit and come back later (not always the case, as it depends how complicated the copy is and how much focus on editing I still have - i.e., I ask myself "am I still wearing the right hat?").

Whatever happens, if I've made any changes at all, it's a signal that the whole piece will need editing again (every change needs a further check - and each check should always be done with fresh eyes).

The problem with long edits (i.e., not the reading part, but the correction part) is that we often need to go back into creative mode. When that happens, we start to see the trees again and miss the forest (i.e., the big picture).

This is why fresh eyes matter. By the time of our last edit, we want to be in a position where we can read the copy from beginning to end without a single glitch, just pure joy for our work.

Common editing conundrums

Adverbs

Adverbs are a big problem for new copywriters. We're taught at school to be creative with our writing, but what that tends to focus us on is the introduction of new words.

Especially, long words that modify or extend shorter, simpler words.

We're also taught that learning new vocabulary is important. We're taught that intelligent people understand far more words than uneducated people - the "hoi polloi" (incidentally, words or phrases like "hoi polloi" are a good example of words we should avoid - anything that makes us reach for the dictionary or scratch our heads is a sign that we're doing something wrong - e.g., we're using difficult words, and need to replace them with simpler or better known ones).

Adverbs are another good example of words to avoid. Adverbs modify or extend verbs or phrases by emphasising them in some way. Adjectives have the same effect but sound less sucky. The problem with adverbs is they can make copy sound amateur or contrived.

You can tell many adverbs by whether they have an 'ly' on the end. Here's an example:

"It becomes obviously clear (and usually is) that any words ending in 'ly' are absolutely to be avoided at all costs especially if your endlessly long copy contains more than a couple of these clearly useless and overly defined words."

If I edit that sentence by removing all adverbs and anything else that obscures the message, I get this:

"Words ending in 'ly' are best avoided."

Clarity

When adverbs and other pointless words are removed from long-winded sentences, we get clarity. Take the following sentence for example:

"If your copy is confusingly obtuse to you in any way, it will certainly be confusingly obtuse to your readers too."

It's clearer if we edit it like so: "If your copy confuses you, it will also confuse your readers."

Arguably both are fine, but there are fewer words, and they're shorter in the second version. This allows our reader to get the message and move on fast (we never want a reader to stumble - which is why we read our copy out loud - if we stumble in any part of it, it's a sign it needs editing).

Speaking of which, I would edit the previous example further and this time use an adverb (shock, horror!):

"If your copy confuses you, it's likely it will confuse your readers too." Note that 'likely' is an adverb - but it also happens to be an adjective (depending on context), either way, I prefer this last version - thus proving that as long as we're aware of the rules, sometimes they're worth breaking.

The bottom line is this: remove words wherever you can to sharpen your writing, but never lose sight of clarity.

Punctuation

We all know how important punctuation is (read the book: "Eats, Shoots and Leaves" by Lynne Truss to convince yourself of that). But by far the biggest mistake made in copywriting is the use of exclamation marks.

Here's the rule: Avoid using exclamation marks, but if you must, never use more than one unless you really want to get someone's attention. Even then, it has to be for a very special reason - such as you believe this will make a big breakthrough (i.e., a massive AHA moment) and you want to ensure they don't miss it (NOTE: Even with that, you won't find me using them - unless it's to make a point about how amateurish they look, like THIS!!!!).

I often miss out question marks (even when it would be grammatically correct to use them). I do this on purpose to mark a rhetorical question, that is, a question where we believe the reader already knows the answer. This is also where exclamations are often used too, e.g., "Can you believe it!", but even here, if you avoid using an exclamation mark or a question mark, it can add more gravitas (seriousness) to it.

Short sentences and paragraphs

Keep sentences short. But note that if every sentence is short, your copy will sound stunted and disjointed, and the flow will fail (this is a common mistake for people just starting out who have learnt this rule and are applying it everywhere).

Traditional books have barely any white space between paragraphs, and paragraphs tend to be long too. Almost every novel is like that. Copy is the opposite. Lots of white space and short paragraphs are the order of the day. By short I mean two or three sentences on average.

The reason is simple. Expectations. When we buy a book, we expect solid slabs of text. But when we read an advert, we know it's there to sell us something, so a solid slab of text puts us off.

There is seemingly an exception to this in the form of long copy in direct marketing ads. The reason they ever worked at all was because they were originally written to mimic the content style of whatever magazine or newspaper they were placed in (the inventor of this style of copy coined the term 'Advertorial' to define it).

These days you'll rarely see this type of advert (they tend to look very dated), but they still crop up from time to time (and presumably, when they do, they still work, but most likely this is because they have been heavily tested first).

Importance of words

At the start of this book I emphasized that EVERY WORD MATTERS. This is a reminder that in the editing process we get a chance to replace some words with better versions of them. 'Better' doesn't mean longer, it means simpler and more to the point.

Instead of using an adverb, ask yourself if there's a better verb or clearer adjective you could use instead. For example: "You can clearly see...." The adverb is 'clearly' the verb is 'see'. If we remove the adverb, we get "You can see...."

Which version is better? It depends, but always prefer a single verb over an adverb. And where you already have a single verb, ask yourself if there's a better verb. For example: "He moved swiftly towards..." could be replaced with "He ran towards..." (thus removing both the verb and

161

the adverb, and replacing them with a clearer, shorter verb
- the sentence no longer sounds amateurish either).

Point of view

Always be aware of your point of view. Is it first, second, or
third person? If so, does the point of view change as the
copy moves along? And if so, are the transitions seamless,
or do they feel awkward?

Most copy is written with a combination of all three. First
person to build trust ('I' or 'my'), Second person to get
personal ('you' or 'yours'), and third person to build proof
('they' or 'them'). See the end of chapter 7 for more
information on the use of pronouns.

Story

Does your copy have a beginning, middle, and end? Are
you taking your reader on a journey? Most journeys in
copy start with the past, then move to the present, and end
with the future (this is for the body copy, the headline is
often future based, but can be both past or present based -
see chapter 9 for more information on headlines).

It's also fine to start your copy by talking about (painting a
picture) of the future. This is usually about the same future
your prospect is urgently searching for. This works well as
long as you pivot back to the past or present so you can
show the difference between where they are now and
where they want to be (and how the product you're
advertising will help them get there).

If your copy has no story, it makes it that much less
interesting. There's one caveat to this. Where you're
advertising to a fully aware audience - they know who you

are and what your product is and does, they probably only want to know about new features and what they will do for them. However, if a brief story helps illustrate it, then there's no reason why you shouldn't include one.

Big idea

Is your big idea clear? Does your copy even have a big idea? (see chapter 7 and also the Rules section and glossary for more on big ideas). Most ads lack a big idea other than leading on price, urgency, popularity, or exclusivity.

There is nothing wrong with that (provided they make a profit), but think how much better any ad would be if more thought was given to coming up with something new or different.

Ideally, your big idea should have been figured out before you wrote the first draft (or, as often happens) whilst you were writing the first draft, so this is more of a reminder that you at least gave it some thought during your draft, and if not, then perhaps see if you can strengthen the copy by introducing one (the point of editing is not just to make copy clearer, but to ensure that important information has been included, and unimportant information excluded).

Flow

Flow is everything. We don't want our readers stumbling around confused or given choices they find hard to make. We want them to fly through our copy and take action. If anything in the copy stops them, we are one step closer to losing a sale. There is a caveat to this though. Sometimes we want them to stop for a second and start thinking about what they've just read. But we only want this to happen if they've just had a Eureka moment. Either way, we want their full attention and their imagination. Speaking of which, if we can get them to fill in the blanks we left on purpose so they start imagining themselves already owning whatever it is we're selling, then our flow is working as it should.

One thing

Does your copy focus on one thing? Ideally, that one thing is your big idea. Copy that introduces one new thing after another can be overwhelming. At some point, our brains can be overloaded, and if that happens, there's a good chance our reader loses attention. It's fine to have different angles and points of interest in your copy, just as long as they all cohesively fit around your one (main) thing.

Emotion

Copy without emotion is everywhere (especially with short ads). The problem is, emotion is the ONLY thing (apart from force) that moves us. As you work through your copy, listen out for your own emotions. What are they? And what made them happen? Is that the effect you want on your readers?

If you're editing someone else's copy, and you find it lacks emotion, it's either because the author decided to ignore emotion on purpose, or more likely, hadn't considered emotion at all. Never make that mistake.

Emotion can be invoked with just one word: Smile. Or even a symbol :)

If you want to move people, ensure your copy a) moves them by using emotional language, and b) changes whatever emotion they might be feeling at the start to whatever emotion you need them to be feeling at the end.

Proof

Check every claim in your copy is supported by proof. Once you've hooked a prospect emotionally, you need to justify it. Any offer without proof will never get close to the sort of returns you can expect when an offer is supported by hard evidence.

To do that, finding credible people you can quote from is ideal. This is why testimonials and social proof work. But if you can't find people to quote from, then a number of different rhetorical devices can be used instead. The first and most common of those is called Allusion. I also use the word 'association' along with this to make some aspects of its power clearer.

Allusion can be used to connect well known people (or other things such as famous products or ideas) with the product or offer you're selling. You can also use allusion to promote or enhance ideas within your copy (i.e., not just promoting the product itself, but features within the product).

For example, it's well known (and often quoted) that Roger Bannister was the first person to run a mile in under four minutes, but if you dig deeper, you'll find he wore a special pair of running shoes, so special in fact, they raised $412,062 when they were auctioned for charity in 2015 (eight times the pre-sale estimate).

The shoes were made from kangaroo hide (who wouldn't want to run that fast!) and had 6 spikes embedded in them. If you were selling running shoes made of kangaroo leather (hopefully from animals that died naturally), this would serve perfectly as a strong allusion to the strength and speed of your product. Of course, if this were a real promotion, you'd also want to explain how you were using the latest technology to enhance them further (or that through some clinical trial you could prove that despite the use of modern materials by other manufacturers, hide was still the best material of all).

A headline for such a product might read: "Proof that Roger Bannister's original running shoes still have the edge over artificial fibres. Why Acme Shoes help you run faster."

Emotive ideas, such as intrigue, work well too. For example: "How a 100 year old technology broke modern day athletic running records."

Using proof through real life stories is also a way of SHOWING what your product can do rather than through simply telling - e.g., "Become the next Roger Bannister" as opposed to "These shoes will help you run faster." (see Show don't tell in chapter 12).

Importance of order

Sometimes what looked like a great piece of copy when drafted can be missing the most important points of all. That is, the answer to the three fundamental questions on every prospect's mind:

1. Why this?
2. Why me?
3. Why now?

This is also known as the "so what!" effect. The more you get used to editing copy, the quicker you'll learn how important this is (especially if you follow the rules outlined in chapter 12, and explained in this chapter).

For example, it's quite common to discover that a paragraph embedded well down the copy would actually work better if it were moved to the top. This is almost always because it answers at least the first two of the above 3 questions, and often all three of them - e.g., "what is so important about this that I should want to read about it now?"

If any paragraph in your copy contains that message (or an allusion to it) and it's not at the top of the copy, the only reason I can think is that the copy is story-based and aimed at a fairly unaware audience. Or to put it another way, the audience needs to be warmed up before we let them know what we are selling and why they need it.

You'll find in practice, especially early on in your career, that this happens a lot. It's another reason why editing matters.

Here's an editing tip I use all the time. Set a timer for 15 minutes for every thousand words you're going to edit. For this book, I set my timer for hourly sessions (but occasionally, 30 minutes). With the timer set, you've given yourself two things: a) a deadline - for my book, I know I'll be done with a session in just one hour, and b) motivation in the form that you'll know you're done when the timer goes off (which will happen soon enough once you're in the editing frame of mind).

11 Prospecting

If you're new to copywriting, don't expect to get any clients (or at least retain them) during your first year UNLESS you are proficient in writing AND you know how to edit your copy to remove ALL mistakes (as outlined in this book).

Any copy you put out that has even a single mistake is a SIGN that you're not the BEST (no one wants to hire average people unless they want average work - and for copywriters who are there to help businesses sell more of what they do, average is NOT what they are looking for). Remember this paragraph. Embed it into your brain. Never forget it.

As I mentioned in chapter 4, if you've been told "good enough is good enough" remove it from your subconscious immediately. As a business owner, I never want to hear that. I want the best for my customers always (because that is their expectation and I want them to return to me again and again).

Anyone who claims good enough is good enough is projecting their own shortcomings in order to placate both themselves AND their customers (or followers).

Obviously, you can only ever be as good as you are at the time, but that's no excuse for shoddy work (e.g., not bothering to triple edit your stuff with a long enough delay in between each edit - at least when you're in your early years as a copywriter).

Perfectionism

Nothing is ever perfect. But it can be as perfect as we are currently capable of. People use the idea of perfectionism as an excuse for not getting stuff done (this is the real reason some people talk about 'good enough is good enough' - but it's not actually helpful).

As I also mentioned in chapter 4 (and worth repeating), perfectionism when used this way (i.e., as an excuse for not completing things) is just another form of procrastination. The reality to getting anything completed is this: do it. When you DO things, things get done. But if you decide you can't do it because of your so-called 'perfectionism' then you are procrastinating.

This is a good thing to know because it allows you to REFRAME the condition in a different way, and sometimes doing that lets us see the road ahead.

There's another way procrastination gets in our way too, and that is when we suddenly realise that we can't complete something until something else is done first, and when we start to do that 'something else', we realise there is another 'something else' to do even before that.

And so it goes on until we just give in because what started out as one problem now consists of many. Luckily for the copywriting profession, the only thing that can stop us is lack of research (and we have Google ready and waiting for that).

So for us, our starting point is research, swiftly followed by writing. Nothing else. Either we're researching and writing copy every day or we're not. Make those your first steps and follow everything discussed not just in this chapter, but every chapter preceding it, and you'll be in a better position than most early-stage copywriters. Doing this will also result in the one thing you're going to need if you want to attract, engage, and convert clients - confidence - read on...

Confidence

The ONLY way you'll get any work in the copywriting industry is to be confident. Confidence comes from EXPERIENCE and nowhere else. All other forms of confidence are tricks. E.g., the idea of being able to "Think and Grow Rich" without doing any work is a trick (it's not provable or disprovable). "Fake it before you make it" is a trick. Avoid tricks at all costs.

If you were to write one 500 word piece of copy every day for a year, you will be able to claim with evidence, confidence and certainty that you have written 365 pieces of copy. That's 182,500 words (or the equivalent of 3 books - and all in just a SINGLE year).

What you won't be able to claim though, is how successful your copy was. If you tried to make something up about how good you were, your confidence will drop due to the lie (for villains this is irrelevant of course, they will do whatever it takes to win regardless of integrity).

You could choose to write those pieces of copy for real world products or services as test pieces. This is fine, but if you do that, make it crystal clear that's what they are, and be very careful about copyright. One way to use this idea is to write pieces for companies you'd like to work with by way of example of what you can do. If your work aligns with what they're after, that could be the break you need.

Portfolio

By creating a series of ads, short, medium, long, and covering different media areas and channels, you're creating a portfolio of work to show prospective clients.

As you create more ads for your portfolio, you will start to discover your inner talents for specific ways to 'show' stories and demonstrate benefits. In short, you will develop your copywriting voice.

The benefit of that will become clear when you first start talking with prospects.

This is all part of the reason why it's important to understand, and fix in your mind, that being a copywriter is not some get rich quick scheme or a fad you'll try for a while then move on to something else if it doesn't work out. You need to decide to be ALL IN on this, and when you do, you'll discover it's the only way to succeed (as with anything worthwhile in life).

Your first customer

There are nearly 8 billion people on planet Earth. It's impossible to say how many businesses there are, but it is possible to estimate it from a quick Google search to around 130 million (there are approximately 32 million businesses in the USA with a population of 331 million - that's around 1 business per 10 people, so our 130 million estimate is a very conservative 1 per 60 people globally).

These figures don't include micro businesses, of which, there are countless more.

If we were to try to figure out the number of GREAT copywriters there are, I can tell you it's tiny in comparison to these numbers. How do I know? Take a look at every ad you see. How do they compare? Does each ad have the attributes you've been going through and that I've explained in this book?

How many ads could you improve? For every ad you think you could make a better job of, it means two things: a) you've just created a good reason why you owe it to that company to reach out to them and show them what you can do (and why it needs to be done if they want to see growth), and b) it's a sign that a good copywriter was not around when these ads were written (i.e., more proof that the world needs better copywriters).

Will they be taking a risk hiring you if you're new? Yes of course. Do they know that? Absolutely. The worst reason you can ever have for not contacting a company you feel you can help is because you think they might think you're not worth it.

Until you contact them, they don't even know you exist, let alone who you are, but worse, they're unaware they need help. So how do you go about finding and contacting them?

In chapter 6, we explored niches and why they matter. Although you may not have picked a niche yet, you will find it helps to do so for one simple reason. Your copy will speak directly to the type of people you want to attract.

Does it mean you're stuck in that one niche forever? No. It just means it becomes part of what you do. It also makes it easier to start the prospecting process.

For example, if you decide you want to focus on technical instrument manufacturers, distributors, or retailers, then it's easy to search Google for, say, "scanning electron microscopes (SEM) for sale."

The results will show you the top players (according to Google) in the SEM industry - and that means the very people we are searching for (manufacturers, distributors, and retailers)

All of them require copywriters. Now ask yourself how many dedicated technical instrument copywriters there are in the world. I just did a quick search on Google, and only one person appeared in the top ten results (it's easy to spy on your competition if you do this too).

Positioning

Check out your competitors' websites and look for who they serve (often to be found in their portfolio or about us page). Now you have a list of prospects, but the real point of seeing who your competitors serve is to discover the TYPE of businesses they write for.

Are the businesses your competitors serve small, medium, or large companies? Are they local, national, or global? What else about them is different? Do they have common factors connecting them together? This is all about research. You need to SEE the market the same way your competitors do (because it's your competitors who are making money from it).

You'll also see how your competitors are positioning themselves in the market. Their home page should say it all. What messages are they sending out to their prospects about what they do and who they serve?

If their messages seem rather general (e.g., "we help you get more leads for less"), how can you be more direct? What is it those companies your competitors are serving really want? Whatever that is becomes your positioning statement.

The more research you do on your market, the clearer you'll get on the sorts of companies who are out there hiring independent copywriters to help them sell more. This will help you search for similar looking companies you can contact as you put together your first list of prospects. Speaking of which, it's time to figure out your pipeline.

Pipeline

Every serious business to business (B2B) company creates a pipeline of prospects. Each prospect they contact is recorded in a database (e.g., a spreadsheet, autoresponder, ERP system, or dedicated prospect management software such as Salesforce, HubSpot, or Pipedrive).

This allows them to create a journey for each prospect to ensure their messages get through to the right person consistently, and keeps them in the loop until the prospect opts out or becomes a customer.

It doesn't stop there though. Every prospect that turns into a customer needs to be handled correctly so they remain a customer (that might mean, for example, giving them special deals from time to time to remind them of the great value you offer, and also, offering them priority services to show that you care enough that you want to recognise and retain them as valued customers).

If you have no budget for dedicated software to control your pipeline, then start with a spreadsheet. Keep this as simple as you can. Every time you find a new prospect, create a new row for them in your spreadsheet. Use the first few columns to add contact details including business name, contact name, email, phone, address, and notes (plus anything else relevant - e.g., their website address and social media accounts).

NOTE: You'll also need to check your country's laws on keeping data of a personal nature to ensure you comply. This includes encryption or other forms of security so that data is kept safe.

The rest of the column headings can be left blank because EVERY prospect will (more or less) have a different journey. So instead of adding headings such as "First Contact Date", "Second Contact Date", add that detail (if necessary) to each field along that prospect's row as you contact each of them in turn.

All that matters at this point is that you know who you should be contacting next, and who you are waiting for replies from. One way to do that is to use a background colour in the first column (their business name) so a quick scan down the list will tell you who needs contacting.

Consider using RED for people you need to contact, YELLOW for people you are waiting on, and GREEN for prospects who have become customers. Why the extra green colour? Because you'll need to use a separate project management tool for every prospect that turns into a customer.

There are two main reasons for using a prospecting tool: firstly, it is to ensure we never run out of customers (not all prospects we turn into customers will stay with us, that's just how business is). Secondly, as your business starts growing, you'll need to find even more prospects.

Your prospecting spreadsheet (or other tool) is different from the tool you'll need to look after customers. To be clear:

A prospecting tool is to find new people who might one day become customers and to ensure we contact them as many times as necessary to remind them we exist and how we can help.

On the other hand, a customer management tool is there to ensure your customers stay customers (because it allows you to manage their projects and campaigns without forgetting important steps, milestones, follow ups, or other todo items agreed to in your contract with them).

Customer and project management

I've used many customer and project management tools in the past including Asana and Trello, but I now use dedicated customer management software to look after projects and tasks. There are many options out there, and many that are free. Start with Trello if you're not sure, it's probably the simplest.

Alternatively you can set up a new tab for customers in your spreadsheet (if that's what you chose as your prospecting tool). However, I find dedicated software easier because everything is set up and ready to go - you just fill in the blanks.

The software I use has 'cards' (similar to the way Trello works). I set up a card for each customer. Then another card for each project for that customer. That way I'm able to research, organise and implement everything necessary to complete each project.

The task cards are placed in columns such as: "Ideas", "ToDo", "Ongoing", "Done", "Abandoned" (these card groups can and do vary by customer and project).

You'll also need to tie this in with a calendar if your tool of choice doesn't include one. Google Docs is a great tool and place to start. It's free, includes automated backups, and syncs with almost everything.

First contact

With your pipeline framework in place, it's time to go prospecting. As mentioned earlier, you can fill your pipeline in many ways, the simplest of which is to focus on a niche and google it to see who the players are (i.e., people active in that field either because they're advertising or because their site is on page one of Google).

The reason we're looking for active people is because they're the ones most likely (and able) to afford (and value) the attention you as a copywriter can give them.

A secondary way is to look for businesses that appear lower down the rankings. There's a reason they're not at the top of Google, and that might be worth exploring with them (this is not about selling yourself as an SEO expert, this is about educating them that using a copywriter will bring them better conversions, and that the extra business brought in that way may well help them to rank higher because they're likely to get more exposure through reviews and social media shares).

I always research companies I'm interested in, and that includes their financials and ownership. Here in the UK, anyone can use Companies House to research registered businesses (and by that I mean limited companies, public companies, and any other bodies that must be legally registered through Companies House - e.g., limited liability partnerships).

I do this to ensure a couple of things. First, that they can afford my fees (this is not a problem when you're just starting out, but will be as you grow), and second, to make sure they're solvent (i.e., not about to be declared bankrupt).

Once you've started populating your pipeline, it's time to make contact. If you were to write a general email and send it to everyone in the list, there's a good chance it will end up in the spam box (and by that, I mean the recipient will hit the spam button the second they think you have no idea who they are).

To get a feel for this, look at what you do to any emails that arrive that seem to have nothing to do with what you need (or want), or that obviously are not personal in nature. If you've ever looked at an email subject line and hit the spam button immediately, that's what I'm talking about.

And if you've opened an email and then hit the spam button after reading the first sentence, that's also what I'm talking about. Your first contact with a prospect is the most important contact of all (if you want to take any prospect further into your sales funnel).

One point to note though: even if they do open your email AND read it without sending it to spam, they are very unlikely to act on it. Why? Because the chances of them being ready AT THAT POINT to order something is rare. Why? Because without researching everything they do including getting an interview with their marketing or sales manager or director, you'll have NO idea what it is they're looking for.

This is just to reinforce how important research is. The more research you do, the better your results.

Introductory email

Your first email is an introduction, but it's an introduction your prospect is neither expecting, nor wants. Bear that in mind.

If you start it with something like "How are you?" it will get binned (unless you already have a highly personal, friendly, and long relationship with them).

Or you could use the old faithful "I'd like to introduce you to my company." That worked well for me for years, but I no longer use it as it feels kind of tired now (it may still work for all I know though - at least it's honest).

The best way is to start with something about their company that PROVES you've done your research. E.g., "Dear ..., After reading about your work on [insert topic], I realised we had a mutual [add some relevant observation], and would love to set up a brief call..."

Don't use what I've written above unless that hits the nail on the head though, by which I mean, avoid cookie cutter email templates - if people think they've seen something before, it can be an instant turn off (I see it all the time in my inbox).

Whatever your suggestion for a call is, make sure it's real and relevant to them, and if you can tie it in with a big idea, so much the better.

Playing field

Consider every pipeline to be a game. And also, that the game runs on a playing field. But not any old playing field, this playing field has three sets of goal posts. The starting point for you are your own goal posts, the starting point for your prospects are their goal posts, and the mutual goal is the third set of goal posts.

Think of the playing field as a triangle with each set of goal posts at the points. Yours are on the bottom left, your prospects on the bottom right, and your mutual goal is at the top.

The idea is to join forces somewhere in the middle so you both reach the top at the same time. It's the perfect win-win situation. It also makes your goal, their goal.

In other words, when you align yourself perfectly with them, everyone wins. When done properly, it also implies you're both not only on the same side, but part of the same team.

It's at this point that they will see a normal playing field with you and them moving forward together to capture as much of the market as they can.

But this can only happen if you do the research and write your email based on that truth (and not some assumption that everyone in your market has the same problem).

If you do make assumptions, you put yourself in the same position as almost everyone else, and then it pretty much all comes down to luck.

First date

It should become clear by now that every email you send should not be some quickly jotted down scribble, but a dedicated piece of copy to persuade or remind someone that a) they have a problem, b) it needs fixing, c) it is fixable, and d) you're the right person for the job.

The problem is, it's never easy telling someone you're meeting for the first time that they have an urgent problem and it needs to be fixed. You'll get rejected out of pure pride if nothing else.

People need (and like) time to let things sink in before they start reacting positively, so our first email must give them that time (along with a reason to want to know more).

To continue with our example introductory email:

"Dear ..., After reading about your work on [insert topic], I realised we had a mutual [add some relevant observation], and would love to set up a brief call at some point as I have some ideas I think you'll find interesting."

That little, almost throwaway, everyday phrase "at some point" is how we give people time. By being non-pushy (which is the same thing as being non-salesy), it stops them from saying "NO" immediately. We're opening the door a little without putting our foot in it.

That brief introductory email is actually a framework. Here's how it works:

1. Always make it personal (e.g., "Dear ...." - always use their name though, NOT something like 'Friend").
2. Mention something at or near the top of their agenda - a project, mission, value, etc.
3. Mention, and if necessary show or imply proof, that you have something in common with the project, mission, or value you just mentioned (this is to show alignment - "we're in this together").
4. Suggest the possibility of a meeting (but with no timeline or commitment).
5. Suggest why that meeting would be useful.
6. Sign off (don't add pressure by concluding with "when would be a convenient time to call?"). This leaves you and them open to further emails.

Email subject line

Just like an ad or landing page, every email needs a subject line, and unless the subject line is interesting, the email has a good chance of being ignored (or going to spam). My advice is to make it detailed. The more it is aligned with something the recipient knows about or is interested in, the more likely it is to be opened.

For example, if you were working on a secret project codenamed 'Cobra' and you received an email from an unknown sender who used the word 'Cobra' in the subject line, you'd certainly want to know more.

Secret or not, it's surprisingly easy to discover what people and their companies are currently involved in by reading their press releases and social media posts. And since most companies want to stand out from the crowd, the best will try to write something interesting. Look for that when researching and you'll always have something useful to get attention and engagement.

Email signatures

Every email needs a signature. What is a signature? Think of it as a shorter version of your 'About us' page. It might include your name, address, and other contact details as well as a link to your site (or even better, a link to a page on your site aligned perfectly with your recipient).

Your email signature might also contain other, more personal details about you, your company, and what you do. And finally, it might contain a bunch of legal jargon. Keep that within the law (obviously - do consult a lawyer) but as short as possible (no one likes to read large blocks of text).

For me, I often change the signature to make it relevant to the recipient. For example, I can use various letters after my name, so if I'm writing to a corporate client, I usually include them. However, if I'm writing to an entrepreneurial or maverick type, I rarely add them, preferring to stick with my first name to sign off, followed by a minimal amount of information.

Send a letter

There is nothing wrong with sending a letter instead. It just takes longer and costs more. However, in my experience, letters are almost always opened and read in comparison to emails.

So whilst email open rates depend almost entirely on the subject line, a letter's open rate depends entirely on the envelope. If it has a hand written name and address plus a postage stamp (and no 'return to sender' info on the back), then it's almost guaranteed to be opened out of curiosity if nothing else.

What to write

With that done, then we come to the contents. Direct response marketers have tried everything, and I can tell you that 'everything' works - but only sometimes. Even envelopes covered in advertising slogans work sometimes (it all depends on audience targeting of course). But we probably don't have the time or money to experiment when we're starting out, so always try the easiest route first (that's why we go for a plain envelope).

There are two approaches you can take with the contents. The easiest is to use what we did for the email. That is, keep it simple. The only difference is how we end the letter. We can't leave it open the way we did with the email because the expectation of receiving a letter asking for a call or meeting is to also include how to make that happen (it's OK not to do this with email, because the expectation is that another email - or something else - will follow, or if we're interested, we can directly reply with a single click).

With a letter, we need to tell them the next step. You have a choice. You can be passive and ask them to contact you ("If this is of interest, please call me when you're free.") or you can be proactive and sign off the letter with something like "I'll call you in a day or two to follow up."

The other approach is to write a full on direct response sales letter outlining everything you'd normally say in a face-to-face conversation. However, since that would be impossible as you don't know them or their likely objections, create a dedicated sales landing page for the industry or niche you're targeting and make a printed letter version of it. Which of these methods you choose is entirely down to how you feel. For me, I prefer the easiest path - and that is to spend more time prospecting than writing long copy sales letters that may or may not work.

Next move

Now you wait. But whilst you're waiting, do the same with all the prospects in your pipeline (in other words, start a new pipeline journey for each prospect). And with that done, find more prospects so you have something to do tomorrow.

Repeat this process every working day (or at a minimum, schedule time for pipeline filling and prospecting every week). If you stop doing this, your pipeline will empty, and whilst you may have work right now, at some point you will need to find new clients.

Whatever you do, the one thing to avoid is ending up with one main client (or you and your business will be at that client's mercy). Should you get into that position, your job is to get out of it by increasing your pipeline work and taking on staff or subcontractors to handle the extra work (and start increasing your rates as you get more of it).

Rejection

Whichever way you decide to create your prospect list, creating a pipeline and making initial contact is the first step in your Customer Acquisition System (CAS). However, it's not all roses. The first problem you'll discover is rejection. It may be immediate in the form of a negative reply, or you may not discover it at all (no reply). But one thing is guaranteed, reaching out to people you don't know will always receive a higher rate of rejection than acceptance. With one exception - cold calling.

Cold calling

Sending an email or letter are two ways of getting attention (even if you don't get a response). Whereas calling people on the phone is a way of GUARANTEEING a response (even unanswered calls tell you something).

The problem with cold calling is that almost everyone hates the phone except outgoing, gregarious people. If you're like me, and prefer writing over calling, I have a solution that will help ease the pain (but you'll still need to pick up the phone - sorry).

The cold calling method I'm about to show still involves sending an email or letter first (just as I've described in this chapter), but we're doing that to give us a legitimate reason to call.

Before I get into what to say, here are the four possible responses we're likely to get to every cold call we make:

1. No answer. The contact is out of the office, on holiday, gone away, or can't be bothered to pick up the phone. This is a signal to try again later (it doesn't have to be during working hours - some of the busiest people in business work late into the night or at dawn).

2. Answerphone. Another signal to try again later. If you leave a message, make it short and simple "This is [insert your name] Sorry to miss you, I'll try again later." Repeat until someone answers (no need to leave a detailed message). DO leave a reasonable gap between calls though - e.g., a day (no one wants to feel like they're being hounded).

3. Someone answers. This may be a gatekeeper (a receptionist or personal secretary). State that you would like to speak to your contact. If they ask what it's about (which most will because they have been instructed to field calls and get rid of any nuisance or waste of time calls) tell them it's about the email or letter you sent about the mission or product you mentioned (if you aligned your content with a value instead of a product, tell them - "I sent an email/letter on Tuesday viz a viz the [insert the value and company name] has."). If they push you on explaining it further, tell them "it's quite detailed and where would they like you to start" (avoid this approach if you can though - it can sound sarcastic, instead just say something like "it's complicated" and ask again for the person). Having said that, the most likely answer will be something like "well I'm

187

sure they will get back to you when they return from their meeting." Don't be put off by any of this. Instead politely ask when would be a good time to call again.

4. Your contact answers. The holy grail. The smaller the company, the more likely this is. The negotiation is now on. The goal is to get a face-to-face meeting (obviously if the company you're calling is not local, then that might be difficult or impossible). Either way, you need to establish if the person has a few minutes right now. How you word that doesn't matter. If they say yes, you're good. If they say no, it allows you to suggest another time "do you have some time today or tomorrow?" This is a closed question (and a double bind so be careful - many people feel uncomfortable with this aggressive style - see double bind in the glossary). If they say they're not interested, say "I'm sorry to have bothered you, thank you for your time." Don't push them any further. The door is still open (plus, you've now officially met, and that is far further than most people ever try for).

Before we go into the negotiation stage, let's continue with what happens if you don't get an answer to follow up calls (or you don't want to make any follow up calls).

Follow up

Assuming you've got nowhere with any of the contacts in your pipeline, you'll need a follow up routine. The old saying is that it takes seven touchpoints to get a reaction. Our first touchpoint was the email or letter. Our second (if you chose to do it) was calling them. The next touchpoint can be anyone of many choices. Here's a list:

1. Another email (it can be about the same thing, or it can be about something new). Whatever you do, don't get pushy (e.g., "I contacted you a couple of days ago and have heard nothing, can you get back to me please!"). Our goal is for happy, long-lasting relationships, and getting pushy is not how that works (dealing with resentful people is never fun).

Email follow ups work best when you have something new to say, but a great way to open your pipeline further is to get them to subscribe to a newsletter.

This is because newsletters achieve a similar purpose, but the crucial point about any follow ups including newsletters is they MUST be relevant AND interesting. If they're not, it won't take long before your emails or newsletters get spammed (this is also why it matters early on in any newsletter style email to let people know how to unsubscribe even if they had no idea they'd been added to a 'list' - i.e., your pipeline).

2. A goody bag. This has been tried a thousand times (and still works - occasionally). If you want attention, send something unusual in the post. Think of your prospect as a close family member or best friend. What would you send them that they would find thoughtful?

If you think about this a little more, you'll start questioning all the freebies you find at live exhibitions and trade shows. Why is it that everyone has free pens, note pads, and trinkets? If you come home with a pocket full of pens, will you remember any of the people you visited? Will the pen remind you of them (assuming you ever get around to using their particular pen) from all the others?

One of my treasured possessions is a shopping trolley keyring token (the type that unlocks supermarket trolleys). I use it every time now. I'll never forget that one company because of that simple trinket.

In the case of using a 'goody bag' as a follow up touchpoint, think about what you could send people that is a) unusual, b) something that they'll actually use, and c) is relevant to what you and they do.

3. Visit them. Obviously this is a costly option (your time) so will only work if they're local, but it's quite astonishing how far you'll get if you turn up (non pushy) and let them know you're local and can help them with their website and marketing needs. If you do this, make sure you research them first so they know you care enough to have found out what they do, what their mission is, and who the people are.

I got my first business off the ground doing this, and that business went on to buy me my first house. In a later business, we used to go round retail chains who stocked our products with a box of doughnuts for the staff asking them how things were going and if they needed any help understanding our products (this included Apple Stores and other major high street retailers - we had to get permission, but that was easy as we already had a relationship with them).

4. Call them. See the previous subsection - 'Cold calling' as well as the next subsection - 'Negotiation' for more details, but this is mentioned again here to let you know that a phone call ALWAYS gets a faster reaction (good or bad) than any other method. Businesses and staff change

over time so even if you were rejected once, it doesn't mean you will be rejected every time.

This also applies to existing customers. The more times you contact them in helpful ways to discuss their business (as always without being pushy) the stronger the relationship will be.

5. Message them. Like cold calling, messaging people you don't know is not the best way to contact people. You need to break the ice first (and gently).

For example, connecting with people on LinkedIn is best done by personalising the connection message in some way (but never do it by brazenly asking for a sale - you will get nowhere fast - and eventually be reported for spam).

Facebook is easier because no connection message is required, and if they accept your friend request, you have a legitimate reason to start chatting, but again, if you go into sales mode, you'll lose.

Once a connection has been made, following up is easy provided you have a plan that does not involve blatant selling, and instead involves engaging with them about their needs.

Researching what they're doing and uncovering what they're working on now is the best path to take. The closer you can get to thinking up a big idea that resonates with them, the more attention they will give you.

This is a good alternative to cold calling on the phone.

6. Retargeting. Retargeting (also known as remarketing) is the name for following up prospects online. This is the most underused method of all (except to online professionals such as media buyers who know how powerful this is).

At the time of writing, you can use Facebook's Ad Library to look into any company that's currently advertising on Facebook. You can see the ads they're currently running, but much more importantly, discover if they're NOT running ads at all.

You can then go to their site and check if they're using a Facebook pixel to track visitors, and if not, then they're missing out on so much potential in terms of sales.

What matters is that YOU should also be using Facebook to track your website visitors so you can retarget them in your own follow up campaigns.

NOTE: this will also help boost your confidence when talking with prospects who need services like this (it doesn't mean you personally have to run Facebook ad campaigns for them, it just means you'll have another way to help them get more business by providing better copy for the ads).

7. Chatbots. Retargeting is not just restricted to the tools Facebook, Google, and other major platforms offer. The use of chatbots (including Facebook's Messenger) are powerful ways of following up not only site visits, but anyone who has clicked on or reacted to your ads in some way.

Although chatbots are typically used most commonly as a first contact point, they work even better when used as a follow up tool. In fact, chatbots can be used as complete sales funnels in themselves (from first contact to buy button).

This is because the technology allows us to build decision trees to filter prospects in any way we please. Here's a typical scenario:

Someone arrives on your site from a Google search for "help with marketing." They're a small family run business with a retail store selling home furnishings looking to see if they can get more visitors to their new online shop.

You have a landing page dedicated to helping exactly those kinds of businesses, and that's where Google sent them (this is why niching down helps). You have installed a Facebook pixel on your site and have instructed it to create a custom audience of visitors (plus, you're also segmenting people who have visited that particular page - the pixel can do amazing things with audiences).

When they hit your landing page, you have the chatbot set up and ready to help them get more from it. For example if they have a question, they can click the bot button and ask away. Or you could set it so it pops up automatically after a certain time period (or when they scroll down to a certain point on the page).

It might ask something like this: "Thanks for visiting the site. To help you further, I can take you quickly to whatever you're interested in. Would you like that?" That's followed with a couple of buttons that read: "Yes, but make it quick" and "No, just browsing."

If they click the YES button, another question follows. For example: "Click whichever option you want..." Up pop a few options such as "I want to know more about content" and "Tell me more about SEO" and so on.

As the visitor clicks further into the sequence, the back end is getting ready to move them to the right spot. On the final question, it might say: "OK. This is what you need" with an option such as "Take me there." And that might lead to another landing page with EXACTLY what they're looking for.

At this point you've made a perfect 'market message match' (i.e., the right message matches with the right market). Since you know the vast majority of people who will arrive here have indicated this is what they want, it makes it easy to create some kind of perfectly aligned opt in gift so you can get their contact details (if not a direct call from them).

It doesn't end there though. You can then follow up by messaging them individually or as a group directly from your chatbot (assuming you have a chatbot with these options).

Why is that important when we can do the same with our email autoresponder? Because almost everyone checks their chat inbox. The open rate for chat is as close as you can get to 100% (compare that to email broadcasts which is often no more than 20-25%).

There is one problem with chatbots though. Never abuse them. Chat only works so well at the moment because the spam rate is considerably lower than email. Hopefully that will stay that way, but we'll have to see.

Negotiation

There are numerous books devoted solely to negotiation. Almost every "How to sell anything to anyone" self-help book is about negotiation. In truth, everything in life is about negotiation, so you might be wondering how such a large topic can be tackled in depth in just a small section of this chapter? What follows is dense, and you may find it worth reading a couple of times so the concepts sink in. It will be worth it.

Every negotiation has two goals - the first is the goal for the negotiator (you), and the second is the goal for the 'negotiated' (your prospect). In most negotiations, your prospect has no idea it's a negotiation until you - the negotiator, reveal it. How and when you do that depends entirely on where you are in your relationship with your prospect.

We need to go back one step though. Negotiation IS communication. There's a reason we say things like "good morning" to each other, and that reason is to state that we're not a threat. Think of it as a proactive self-defence mechanism. If we pre-empt any form of possible attack (real or perceived) we feel safer.

That may sound a little over the top, but that doesn't make it any less true. The goal of phrases like "good morning" can also be used to start or warm up a relationship (which, in reality, is much the same thing as our proactive self-defence mechanism). The real point of ALL talk is to achieve something, which is good to know, as there's always a motive.

Motives vary widely. It could be as simple as loneliness (which is also survival), but whatever the motive, it's always a result of something needed or wanted, and if successful, then the goal is achieved.

There are two premises here:

1) All communication is a negotiation of some sort.

2) All communication has a motive (and therefore a goal).

Once you fix these two premises firmly in your mind, you'll realise just how important all conversations are, and this will get you in the right frame of mind for everything that follows on negotiation and winning deals.

Desperation

All animals have a strong sense of fear. We've all heard the notion that animals can smell fear, and from the many studies published on this, we now know it to be true (we release certain pheromones under certain conditions). But there are other signs of fear, not least of which is body language including physical features such as the way we talk.

When predatory animals smell fear in their prey, it's a signal to attack. When a human detects fear in someone they're negotiating with, it's a signal to do the opposite - walk away.

Fear comes in many forms, but the biggest fear of all when it comes to negotiation is desperation.

Desperation is a sign that things are not right, and when it's coming from the negotiator (e.g., us trying to convince someone to use our copywriting service) it raises the question in a prospect's mind that whatever is being sold here is probably best avoided.

Knowing that we need to avoid desperation at all costs is one thing, but what's the alternative if we feel desperate? It's confidence. Confidence = sales. Desperation = no sales.

If you remember nothing else about negotiating, remember the two premises and this one thing, it will stand you in very good stead.

As stated earlier in this chapter, confidence comes with knowledge, but the best knowledge comes from direct experience. The problem for most people is not the gaining of knowledge, it's the gaining of experience.

How to gain confidence

For copywriters, there are three ways to gain confidence:

1) Write copy.

2) Use your copy to sell your own products.

3) Use your copy to sell a prospect's products.

The first two are easy (you just go and do it - it's how I started). But there's more to the third way than you may at first realise, and it's this:

You don't need to find and convince any prospects in order to sell their products.

You can do it with affiliate sales. There are countless organisations you can sign up with to start promoting other people's products. Perhaps the best known is Commission Junction (or CJ Affiliates as they now market themselves as).

You get to pick whatever it is you fancy promoting, write the copy (a quick online search will show you how others are promoting it to help you with research), and then either create an SEO style landing page in the hope that the search engines will pick it up, or if you have a budget, pay for ads to promote it.

I highly recommend using ads since it will give you the fastest and most reliable results and will be a direct reflection of your copy skills.

As long as you get sales, you'll now have solid proof you can use to convince any prospects that you know what you're talking about (even if they're not the manufacturers or distributors of the products you've sold).

And even if you fail to make a single sale, you can at least legitimately state you have written copy for such and such brands. Not making sales will NOT help your confidence though, so it is in your best interests to make your copy work (any successful company with a proven affiliate scheme is making money, so there's no reason you shouldn't be a part of that success).

It's the same thing with number 2 in our confidence building list (selling your own products). It can be as simple as promoting an eBook you've written.

But without doing any of those things, including number 1 (writing copy), your confidence will be almost zero when it comes to talking with prospects, so building this into your plan is perhaps the best advice there is when it comes to prospecting and negotiations.

Remember too, that this is proof you can use on your site as part of your own online marketing efforts and positioning. This is how you get real hands-on experience in the copywriting industry on your own terms - write ads that sell products.

Always be asking questions

Earlier we talked about the options you have when calling your prospects for the first time (this includes following up affiliate sales calls with your vendors if you chose that way to gain experience).

There is one rule you must keep in mind at all times though when talking with prospects. This is ALL about them and NOT you. It's the easiest thing in the world to start talking about yourself in any conversation, but your prospect doesn't care about you. They only care about themselves.

The question is, how do you go about allowing them to talk when you know almost nothing about them and they know almost nothing about you?

The answer is one of my core negotiation rules: "Always be asking questions." As soon as you start asking questions about THEIR business, they'll find it almost impossible to say no (provided the questions are genuine and have no obvious ulterior motives).

Here's an example introduction: "Hi, I heard about you from XYZ who said you'd been in the ABC business for XX years. It's something I too have been involved with and I'd love to talk about how you got started as I'm writing a post on the industry for my blog. I realise you're super busy, but would it be possible at some point to briefly talk with you?"

This is not a template for you to use (although you're welcome to use it), just an example of how you might go about showing interest in what they're doing as a way to both introduce yourself and get them interested in talking.

As I say, this MUST be genuine. We're not here to trick people into a conversation (we'll leave that to the cowboys and villains). If you were to use the above example, then you need to make it part of your marketing plan - which also means figuring out what value there is in writing a blog about the prospect's business.

I have written blog posts that rank at the top of Google for specifically this purpose. I've had phone calls with companies as a result of doing this. It doesn't mean they become clients (although some will). The point is a quicker path past gatekeepers and other obstacles.

The more we know about the people we want as clients, the easier any negotiation becomes.

What to say next

We now know how to introduce ourselves (make it all about them, not us), but what's next? More questions. What questions? Questions that carefully take your prospect along the path they need to go on to become more interested in everything you're asking them about.

For example, I had a client in the bathroom industry a few years ago. I researched as much as I could about him and his company before we talked on the phone. I knew his website had many issues, so my first step was to discover how much he knew about it (or whether he was even interested in increasing his online presence).

It turned out he didn't care much, but was certainly open to be convinced of any merit a larger online presence would have. We agreed to a face-to-face meeting so I carried out a site audit before we met.

I showed him some basic online aspects he was missing out on, the largest being an almost zero Google presence (and not just for his site, but for assets such as a Google My Business listing). There was also no presence on Bing either. There was a minor presence on Facebook, but that was pretty much it for social media.

All of these channels require content, and since I had plenty of proof on what content was needed to bring in more traffic (just by researching his competitors), it was exceedingly easy to ask the most obvious questions, such as "if we could increase your online traffic, do you think it might help bring in more phone calls?"

You'll soon discover that prospects either become highly interested (in which case they go along with your every suggestion), or they become bored. In the latter case, you'll find it almost impossible to reverse that, so my best advice is to end the meeting as soon as you can and exit.

Twenty questions

Think of negotiation in the same way people think about the game twenty questions. We have to find the most direct path to the answer or we lose. There's no time for boredom (unless we have no idea what questions to ask).

Your job as chief negotiator is to discover as fast as possible the most important problem your prospect has. That is, the problem that is currently top of their mind. If it turns out to be something you can't help them with (e.g., they're growing so fast, they're desperately in need of new staff), then back off immediately. Better they forget about you fast than pigeonhole you as a nuisance.

By backing off early, you leave the door open to future negotiations should you see a change in their needs (they will remember you as being non-pushy - and that's what you want from every negotiation including those for which you were rejected).

Listen

The other side to asking questions is listening. We've all been told this many times of course, but even so, most of us are lousy listeners. My worst habit was 'stealing' someone's power when they told me a story I could relate to. My response was always to start telling my own version of it (e.g., "I had the exact same thing happen to me, let me tell you about it...").

Our prospects don't want to know anything about us except one thing: can we fix their burning desperate issue. The rule is, we, the negotiators, ask the questions, and then we let them answer how they please. This is how to win trust.

As they're describing whatever it is we've asked them about, listen very carefully to the parts that resonate with how you can help. No need to say anything yet, just note it down (I always carry a notebook with me to every meeting - not electronic, just a notepad and pen - I find it more reliable, faster, and less intrusive).

At certain points, they may well start asking you questions. Keep your replies as short as you can. Always be as polite as you can, and always be sincere. Return the focus back to them as soon as possible (keep remembering we're here to help them not us - that comes later).

Be ready to chip in only if the conversation veers off to some random topic that has nothing to do with their problem. I've made the mistake many times of letting prospects ramble on about something irrelevant to their business. Don't mistake this with being rude, this conversation is about their problems, and we would be doing them a disservice to not keep them on the problem/solution path (they'll appreciate it all the more if you bring their focus back with something like "Oh, I can see that very well, now how does this relate to the problem of xyz?" - it's very important you don't sound sarcastic though! - mean what you say, and you won't).

Doctor

One of the best pieces of advice I've ever been told was "Be The Doctor." Doctors don't mess about (they don't have the time and they have nothing to sell - at least where I live in the UK).

Doctors also care about their patients (well, most do), and that forms part of the trust and bond we have with them. If you ever meet a doctor you don't like, let that be a reminder of how NOT to behave with clients.

Having said that, most private medical practices have strong ethics when it comes to selling and recommendations (not least, because they don't want to be sued), so remembering to put on your "doctor's hat" will put you in the right frame of mind.

To get a patient to reveal the clues needed to diagnose their problem, a doctor starts by asking about the symptoms. As patients, most of us have no idea what's really wrong. All we know is we have a headache, a pain somewhere, or we just feel ill.

Think of symptoms as unwrapping an onion. The heart of the matter is at the centre. To get there we need to peel off the surrounding layers. Those layers represent the symptoms, and once we reveal each layer, the problem becomes clear. Each question we ask is based on the answer we got to the previous question.

For example, we might start by saying something like: "So I know your website is not performing as you'd like, have you any idea why?" They might reply: "Not really, although

I can see it's because I'm probably not getting enough traffic." That's the outer layer removed.

We'd follow this with question 2: "So if you were to get more traffic, do you think that would really help?" The reply might be: "Well, I'm not so sure. Even when I did have traffic, it still didn't seem to do much good." That's layer 2 removed.

We might follow that up with: "So maybe if you were to get a better class of traffic, that is, people who were actually interested in what you sell, that might help?" The reply might be: "Yes. That would help for certain."

And now we know the problem (wrong kind of traffic) and the solution (get more qualified traffic), so we're ready to start the negotiation proper.

Before we go there, there's one vital piece of knowledge you MUST keep in mind during every negotiation. It's about price.

Price

Remember this one golden selling rule:

Never reveal the price until you're certain they appreciate the value.

If, as sometimes happens, they kick right off with something like "can you give me a rough idea of the cost?" reply without hesitation "that's impossible to work out until I understand exactly what you need to get you to where you want to be" (or something along those lines). Again, sincerity is everything here. You MUST believe that (not least, because it's true - how can you price something if you don't know what's involved?).

If they reply with something like "Oh sure, I understand that, but can you just give me some indication of what a business like mine would pay for XYZ?", you have two choices. Say the same line again, or (and I sometimes do this), give them a figure. The latter method is a good way to pre-qualify prospects without sounding salesy but ONLY if they asked about price first.

Prequalifying

On the same point, if you only want to work with high paying clients, reply with something like "well, a typical business like yours would need [insert number] of articles added to your site every month, along with quarterly ad campaigns including opt in forms, landing pages, email sequences, and retargeting, plus ad management, and that would typically cost around [insert your charges] not including ad spend. But let's find out exactly what you need first..."

Again, this is not some set script, it's just an example of the sort of angle to counter people who want to know the price before they've understood the value (i.e., the value of what it's worth to them to have someone solve all their problems).

Any prospect who starts by asking about the cost, fits into one of two categories. The first is they already know what they want and how much they're willing to pay, the second is that they're very short of funds and don't want to waste anyone's time by discovering early if the price is beyond their budget.

This is why pre-qualifying is sometimes a good idea if you want to avoid problem clients (it's also useful if you want to find clients for whom money is less of a problem than finding the right person).

In general though, never talk about the cost or price until you know what they want and you're certain you can deliver it. If they like what they're hearing from you, and agree (in principle) that this is what they want, the next step is to outline the scope of work.

You have a choice at this point. 1) explain that you want to work on a detailed plan and fix a date for your next meeting, or 2) go for a broad outline, check again that's exactly what they want, and then ask how they'd like to proceed. This is an invitation for them to ask for the cost (and by the way, ALWAYS use the word COST, not PRICE - the cost is how much something is worth, the price is how much someone is willing to pay, there's a big difference psychologically, and it applies to both negotiator and negotiated - i.e., you and your prospect).

Scope of work

You cannot price anything without knowing how much work is involved. Your prospect will only understand that if you make it clear to them. Luckily, it's the simplest thing in the world to do, and it starts by talking about results.

The more valuable the result is for them, the higher the value of the work. This is why the majority of your conversations/negotiations will be about what they want from this, that is, the value you want to get across should be anchored on the end results, not how it's achieved.

The details of how you're going to achieve that can be set down in a plan or left unset. How much of the plan you need to show them depends entirely on their interest in seeing it. For most clients, you will find (as I have) that it's minimal.

This is for two reasons. Firstly, if you focus on results instead of implementation, that influences and forms their front of mind thoughts. Second, if you've won enough trust, they won't need you to explain what you do in detail.

What matters is NOT that you don't want to explain what you do in detail, but that you don't want to bore them. If you've agreed results and expectations clearly enough for both of you to understand your role, then you're duty bound to deliver on them. The prospect is taking a risk, and understands as well as you do, that if you don't deliver, then your work with them will end pretty fast.

In short, the scope of work represents the Key Performance Indicators (KPI's) of a project. A KPI is the expected or required outcome. If a prospect has calculated that a particular KPI is worth such and such an amount, then your fees, provided they are lower, become a no-brainer.

Pricing a job

You can charge in a huge number of ways, but ultimately it comes down to this:

1) Time or other KPI based rate (e.g., cost per hour or cost per word).

2) Project based rate.

I always choose option 2 as a preference, however, there are times when option 1 makes sense. For example, I also host sites for some clients, and for that I make a recurring (usually monthly) fixed charge (depending on their likely resource usage).

Whichever method you choose, working out how much you need to charge is a simple matter when you base it on your needs (not your wants). Most copywriting work has zero overhead cost other than your time (assuming you don't rent office space).

So start by working out how much you need to live your life. Supposing that's £5000 a month. Now figure out how many hours you want to work per month. Let's say it's 160 hours. Divide the amount you want by the amount of time you're willing to work to get it and you'll get your hourly minimum cost (in this example it will be 5000 / 160 = £31.25 per hour).

That means if someone asks you to write a 5000 word sales page, and you reckon it will take you 20 hours including research time, editing, and revisions, you can tell them the cost is £625. There's no need to tell them how you came to that figure (but if they ask, you should of course do so in the simplest possible way - "I charge £31.25 per hour and I reckon this will take me 20 hours including research, editing, and revision.").

What this method fails to do though, is take into account the times you won't be working. That is, when you have no work to do, or you decide to go on holiday, or you get sick, or any number of other reasons. This is the same for every business, so most people choose to add in a multiplication factor to compensate. For example, if you budget for only working 80 hours a month instead of the 160, then you'll need to double your charge to £62.50 (using our example numbers).

All I advise is that you don't get greedy. Focus on your clients' needs first. The more you do that, the more likely you'll get the work you need to sustain your business.

Every conversation

Every conversation is different, but the more you have, the more you'll detect certain patterns. For example, you'll quickly discover how desperate you are by the number of rejections you get (and by listening to the points at which your conversations change - that is, listen carefully to when you lose your prospect's attention - and should that happen, know it's a signal for you to stop talking and bring them back into the conversation with questions such as: "how does that sound so far?" or "does that make sense?" or "is there anything on your mind?").

One last point: the so-called close

In the 1992 film Glengarry Glen Ross, Alec Baldwin lays into Jack Lemmon and the rest of the salespeople with the simple statement: "Always Be Closing" (or ABC). If you haven't seen the film, it's worth watching for the acting alone. But as for ABC? Forget it. Leave ABC to the snake oil salespeople out there.

It does get results, but that's because it's pushy as hell. You'll never grow any long-term relationships with this method (and if you do get clients, they will be hard to maintain for many reasons including refunds/mis-selling battles - or just downright refusals to pay).

ABC was fine back in the days of no internet and social media because it was hard to leave reviews anywhere, but things are very different nowadays, so even if you have zero ethics, ABC is still a bad idea.

Keep a journal

Every time you have a conversation with a prospect you learn something new. I strongly suggest you keep some kind of diary for those conversations. In particular, note any turning points. Record your emotions. Record your prospects' reactions. Record the outcomes. Then ask yourself these questions:

1. "Did I do the research?"
2. "Did I go in with intent?"
3. "Was I in any way desperate?"
4. "Who did most of the talking?"
5. "Did I discover their front of mind problem, then peel back the layers?"
6. "At what point did they ask about price?"
7. "How did I make first contact?"
8. "What follow ups did I do that resulted in this meeting?"
9. "Did they say or reveal anything that I found surprising?"
10. "Was there anything I regretted saying or doing during the conversation?"
11. "What was the outcome?"

The more conversations you have, the more questions you can add here (or revise those that already exist). Use these questions as the basis for your diary (you don't need to answer every question, but the more you answer, the better you'll get at prospecting and negotiation).

Hopefully, you now have all you need to help you on your way to becoming a top professional copywriter. The rest of this book covers various elements to remind you of important concepts and definitions of different terms and frameworks.

PS. One thing I haven't mentioned yet is leverage. Every piece of copy that ever sold anything is called the 'control' or 'control piece' (see chapter 9). If a better piece of copy comes along that beats the control (in terms of overall revenue, net revenue, or conversion factors, etc.), that piece becomes the new control (and the old one is discarded). Few people in business know this terminology, which makes it a great example of leverage. Use it to win clients by asking them how their current sales copy is working out, suggesting that if you were to take over, you would create copy that outperforms what they currently have (and thereby become their new best friend).

12 Rules

There are reasons why some copy works. The most obvious is clear language. If a sentence is in ANY way complicated or hard to understand it will interrupt your audience's flow. Depending on how bad that interrupt is, there's a chance they may give up and leave.

But there's another major reason for copy to fail, and that's boredom. A sentence MUST command attention or the reader will leave.

The purpose of copywriting is to make sales, but without getting our prospects' attention, and holding it, they will never read far enough to see the benefits no matter how well we write them.

This applies as much to you attracting and converting prospects for your own business as it does to attracting and converting customers for your clients' businesses.

If you can write an ad so compelling it brings you clients, then you can happily claim the ability to do the same for them. If you can't, then you have no right to make that claim. But that's solvable, and it starts by learning the rules.

What are the rules?

Unless you know the rules (and when to break them), your copy will NEVER be as effective as it could be. No matter how good you are at negotiating deals, when it comes to delivering the goods (i.e., copy that converts), your clients will leave you in droves if your copy fails to convert (and leave you with reputation damage too).

The gurus tell us rules are there to be broken. We've all heard it, but how do they know? Every rule was made by a human. Humans are fallible. If there's a mistake to be made, we will make it.

Every rule ever created is a rule of its time. As we learn more about life and human behaviour, rules change. What works one day may well stop working the next.

For example, in the Internet Marketing (IM) industry (where almost every price seems to end in a 7), IM copywriters often ask: "why 7?" No one can answer this. It probably came about because some people consider 7 to be a lucky number.

Once someone became successful with this price tactic, everyone copied it, and now price points in the IM market start at $7 and end at around $9997. It's the only market out there that uses this tactic. Every other industry in the West uses a zero or nine almost all the time.

However, the choice of 9 in the retail world didn't happen by chance. It came as a result of research. Products priced $9.99 outsold the same products priced at $10. There was science behind it, and even today, that same science works.

When we see $9.99 we see $9. When we see $10 we see $10. We perceive the difference as 10%, when in fact it's a hundred times less (1p not $1).

Today, the 9 rule about pricing remains. As the IM industry matures, you'll see them come into line (it's happening already amongst some of those moving away from the dodgier IM tactics of old).

There are many rules that have never changed though (so far). The following is a list of them with explanations why they still matter (and in some cases, with exceptions). The more you learn and practice them, the better you will become (not just as a copywriter, but as a writer in general).

1 Every word matters

You already know that every word matters, but I really do mean EVERY word. It's not just important words like verbs, adjectives, and nouns, it's EVERY SINGLE word in EVERY piece of copy. You'll discover this the more editing you do (changing even one word in a sentence may result in the need to change many other words too, and it can often mean rewriting the entire sentence, paragraph or even section).

That means you cannot write great copy without ensuring every word is there for a reason. Irrelevant words are superfluous and must be edited out or the reader will get bored (and we know the consequences of that).

But it's not just the removal of irrelevant words. Explaining the same thing over and over may work if a concept is hard to grasp (because we're dealing with an unaware audience, say), but labouring over the same point just adds fluff.

2 Don't be precious

When we first start writing (any kind of writing) we become precious about it. We often start a special document dedicated to saving those precious sentences we loved but never used (just in case). Yet in practice, we mostly, never look at them again.

So I urge you to learn to write stuff and delete it with joy. Trust in your ability to improve yourself every day. It will happen. The more you write the better you get. The hard part (at first) is deciding WHAT to write.

That's actually easy. Pick any object around your office or home and write about it. Write anything. Describe it in detail. Describe its features. Write why those features matter (the benefits). Write why you bought it (or why you think someone else bought it). Think about how much it's worth. Explain why it's worth it. But above all, do this every day so you get used to doing it (turn it into a habit).

Then, at the end of each session, throw away your copy (you'll find that exceedingly hard to do at first). The more you do this, the easier it will become (and the better you will write).

NOTE: I'm only talking about throwing away practice copy :)

3 Use short words

If nothing else, always do this. We never want our readers to trip up just because we found the perfect word, but which required the average reader to dip into the dictionary to check its meaning.

If you ever suspect a word you've used is not well known enough, edit it out with something simpler. Break this rule at your peril.

NOTE: Use one of the many free grammar checking tools to check your copy's Flesch Kincaid rating if you're in any doubt about your choice of words. We want our copy to be read as easily by adults as children. An ideal score is 80+.

Exception 1: If the copy is for an expert audience who expect certain words to be used, then you need to respect their needs. However, also remember that they too need to be able to get through a document without having to scratch their heads.

Exception 2: Sometimes only one word will do. If you know it suits your audience and they won't need to look it up, use it. You can also ensure that ONLY the right audience you want stays by using longer, perhaps more complicated words. Either way, remember the first rule - every word matters.

4 Avoid adverbs

If you inadvertently use words that end in 'ly' (e.g., ironically and inadvertently), try totally removing them entirely (< see what I did there) and see if the sentence is clearer.

Most adverbs end in 'ly' - but not all. For example, the word 'some' when used in a phrase such as "to some extent" becomes an adverb (whereas, in the phrase "some fish" it's called a determiner - that's because we're not sure how many fish, but we need a way to say we're not sure, so in the latter context, 'some' is OK).

Get used to looking up words in Google by prefixing them with 'define' (e.g., search for: 'define some'). The more you do this, the better you'll understand words (and if it's true that 'every word matters' then it makes sense that you'll find this an important habit to start).

Sometimes it's OK to use adverbs though, so what exactly are they? Here's the definition according to Google: "a word or phrase that modifies or qualifies an adjective, verb, or other adverb or a word group."

The important word in that definition is 'modifies'. With careful thought, you'll often find you can replace the verb being modified with a better verb (and so can remove the adverb entirely - note that the word 'entirely' is also an adverb and can be removed from this sentence as it's totally pointless - as is the adverb totally - as is also the adverb 'often' used earlier in this paragraph).

In short, if you find removing a word in a sentence doesn't change the sentence's meaning, it will almost certainly be an adverb (or an adjective - which can also often be removed).

5 The attention rule

Without attention we have nothing. Attention starts with the first word and should continue to the first sentence, the second sentence, the first paragraph, the second paragraph, and so on right to the end.

At no time must attention be lost or the copy starts to fail. When your words command attention from the beginning to the end it works. Copy like that can be any length. The only rule for how long-copy should be is the attention rule.

Remember this often quoted phrase: The point of the first sentence is to get the reader to read the second sentence. The point of the second sentence is to get the reader to read the third sentence until all the sentences in the first paragraph have been read. So making the point of the first paragraph to get the reader to read the second paragraph and so on.

It makes sense then that the point of a headline is to get the reader to read the first sentence (and the point of any graphic or image in an ad is to get the reader to read the headline).

6 Keep it personal

Every piece of long copy needs a point of view. If we can't identify with the copy, we won't know who we're listening to (and when we don't know who we're listening to, we take less notice).

To that end, you have a choice. Use pronouns or not. There are three to think about and they tie in with something called Point of View (POV).

If I talk about ME, it's coming from MY point of view. That's called first person POV. If I talk about YOU, it's coming from my point of view on what I think matters to YOU. That's called second person POV. If I talk about HE, THEM or THEY, it is called third person POV.

I, you, he, she, them, they, are all examples of pronouns, and they all matter deeply in copywriting (note the use of the adverb 'deeply' - sometimes adverbs do matter - but only when used intentionally - rules can always be broken if thought about with intent).

The best copy 'talks' to the reader as though they were there with the writer having a one to one conversation. This is because all our relationships work this way. We're used to it, and we trust it.

Using 'I' is fine, but if the copy only uses 'I' without a hint of 'you', 'them', or 'they', it will almost always fail.

There is an exception to the sole use of 'I', and that is a personal testimonial or autobiographical copy used to help or support people to take action. With those, first person POV is vital and expected.

Note also that copy that ONLY uses 'you' or 'your' can get tedious, overbearing, and patronising. You'll know if that's the case by following rule 7.

7 Read it aloud

Why is it when some people speak, they sound convincing? It's because they are being themselves. But don't worry if you think that's not you, you can retrain yourself to become just as effective.

How? - by writing carefully crafted copy, then reading it aloud. How will you know you've written carefully crafted copy? Because, when you read it aloud to yourself, you will hear just how sucky it sounds if it isn't.

In other words, carefully crafted copy means it sounds great to hear.

The trick is to listen to your own groans as you read it aloud. Every time you feel something isn't right, make a note of it in your text. They will be the places that need fixing. Practice this for at least your first year (eventually you'll be able to do it in your head).

8 Find your big idea

Every great piece of copy has a big idea behind it (see chapter 7 How to write commanding copy). No big idea, no deal. It's the easiest thing in the world to write a boring ad. Just copy what everyone else is doing. The trouble is, you'll always be second - and no one remembers who came second.

A big idea doesn't have to be huge, just different to what came before. People always prefer NEW to old (even if the only thing that's new is the use of the word 'new' - no matter how unethical that may be).

A big idea can be anything from a new slogan to a new feature to a new benefit, to something completely imaginary that any of those things conjure up (and everything else that you can dream up that makes something be, or appear to be, different).

Volkswagen's slogan of the 1950's was 'Think Small'. Apple's famous slogan of the 1980's was Think Different™.

Find a big idea for each piece of copy you write. Avoid using the same idea twice unless you can find different angles to work around. Once a big idea has run its course (because sales start declining) it's time to find a new one.

Sometimes a big idea can be reused over and over and last a lifetime (L'Oréal's "Because You're Worth It" and Tesco's "Every Little Helps" are two examples of many).

9 Stick to one thing

Apart from the many problems you see with copy that breaks all the rules covered so far, the biggest is not sticking to a theme (or big idea).

Some copy introduces so many features, advantages, and benefits (see FAB in the glossary), it becomes confusing to the reader.

That's also the most common mistake made by marketers in general. They try to cover everything anyone could possibly want. The result is a confused buyer.

If I want a copywriter who specialises in the health industry, I do not also want someone who can build websites, create videos, ghost write novels, or rewire my house.

When copy sticks to one thing and never veers off to other topics, its readers are never confused. They know what it is, who it's for, what it does, and why they need it now.

There's nothing wrong with highlighting multiple benefits - you'll need to - just make sure they all fit in with your big idea and the one thing theme.

10 Make it emotional

The best copy draws us into the scene (just like any good story or film). Before we know it, we're right there in the action, no longer reading the words, but imagining ourselves using the product or service and seeing how it can change our lives for the better.

Be warned though, if anything is out of place, we're pulled right back into the real world. We see the copy for what it is - a way to take our money, and from that point on, it's almost impossible to return.

Making copy emotional is achieved by showing people their new world and what it would feel like if they were in it. If I TELL you that winning the lottery means you get a big pile of money, it means nothing. But if I SHOW you what that WORLD OF MONEY looks like, then your emotions and desire will rise (see rule 12).

Emotion is the ONLY thing that moves us (other than force). But emotion alone is not enough. At some point, logic is required to PROVE our claims. That makes emotion the mover and logic the closer. One without the other always fails.

11 Don't promise what you cannot deliver

This should go without saying, but unfortunately, in the copywriting world, it happens all too frequently, and whilst it does pull in the gullible, over-promising results in long-term losses of both money and reputation.

The satisfaction of writing a great, truthful ad that highlights (with proof) the benefit most wanted by that audience outweighs any amount of over-promising in the ad's copy.

Systems thinking (see chapter 7 How to write commanding copy) is how we know this to be true. The sale of a product is not a system, it's what happens, before, during, and especially afterwards that makes the difference between a short and long-term business.

12 Show don't tell

Compare these two sentences. "Let me tell you how to..." versus "Let me show you how to..." The first reminds most of us of being told what to do. We hate it because, inevitably, as a child, we got told off if we didn't do as we were told.

But to be given the option of being SHOWN what to do, is not just helpful, it helps us trust the person doing the showing because we immediately know they're there to help us.

This can be achieved with the written word, and when done well, keeps the audience on our side. We become the trusted advisor (not the boring bully).

But there's more to showing than that. When we show things, we're describing the experience not just the features.

"This car includes a fully electric transmission system, electric windows, seats and pretty much everything else. Plus it has 100% green credentials."

I've just TOLD you the most important things about this car. If I add the benefits, I will also be SHOWING you what's possible.

"This car includes a fully electric transmission system so you'll never have to pay through the nose again for fuel. It also features electric everything else, so opening windows,

adjusting seats and setting it up ready for you to drive can all be achieved with a single click of a button. Plus its 100% green credentials ensure you'll be doing your bit for the planet too."

There's another side to showing that novelists use all the time. Instead of describing a scene, they describe something within the scene that implies something ABOUT the scene.

For example: "The temperature was 40 degrees inside the car." Let's rewrite this using a "show not tell" approach: "John wound down the window to let in some cool air as he started on what would be a long hot journey."

Showing is about action and dramatization. Telling is about description. We want the reader to feel they're in the room carrying out the action. I highly recommend Janice Hardy's book ("Show, Don't Tell"), especially if you're also interested in creative writing.

13 Appendices

Appendix A - Objection handling

If someone is aware of what they want, including what it is, what it does, and what it costs, they will have few objections when offered it. But of the few objections they might have had, trust will be top of the list. So if they trust the seller 100% and everything else is just right, then they will buy.

However, if they still turn it down, then the seller is going to need to discover and handle each and every objection until the buyer is 100% convinced this is the right deal and that no one else can beat it no matter what they say.

Get your objection handling right though, and there's an even bigger plus side to this - people will often pay more for something because they not only trust the seller, they like the seller too.

That can also happen because of the 'convenience factor'. Going somewhere else costs time and money. This tells us that the margin depends very much on whether getting it done here and now will save them more in terms of time, money, and effort than going elsewhere.

In terms of copy, this is a big deal. Some of the world's largest corporations work this way. They've always understood the value of the trust factor, but they also know the convenience factor adds influence.

This can work in reverse too. If we know that we can buy some product from our favourite, most trusted store, but they are out of stock, depending on our desperation or desire for the product, we are more than capable of lowering our standards (as buyers) to get it.

All of these factors need to be taken into consideration when writing copy, and that means understanding exactly who our audience is.

Objections never appear all at once. They come in serially, one at a time (one objection often follows another especially if the first is not handled correctly).

To discover objections, we need to put ourselves in the shoes of our prospects and read through our copy. To do that we need to know our prospect. It's impossible to know anyone completely (even ourselves), but nevertheless, we must get as close as we can.

For example, if we know they are sceptical, we need to reassure them from the start they can trust us and the product. If we know they are budget conscious we need to either face that straight on, or better still, show the value before any discussion about price appears in the copy,

Think about how many adverts' biggest selling points are often about some sale or huge discount. There's nothing wrong with that, but it will only work on people who already know what they want and who are in the market to buy it now (in other words, the most aware people).

The most common objections

1. I can't afford it
2. I can't afford it right now
3. I don't have the money

4. It's not for me
5. I need to talk to my partner/colleague/manager etc.
6. Send me more information
7. It doesn't do what I want
8. I already have a deal
9. I'll think about it
10. It's not a good time

These are only the tip of the iceberg when it comes to objections (or excuses). But there's more to objections than meets the eye, and we call that the 'objection problem'.

The objection problem

Often the stated objection is not the real objection. It's a cover to save face (or get out of the conversation without having to explain what the real problem is). A great example is "I can't afford this right now." It feels like a show stopper, yet, when the desire is strong enough (i.e., it becomes a passion), almost nothing will stop a transaction from taking place - the prospect will do everything they can to secure the funding.

To prove that to yourself, think back to a time when you "just had to have that." What steps did you take to find (or justify) the money and secure it? Obviously this won't apply to everyone, but it's a useful exercise to see how passion can drive sales (and a reminder of the need to build desire in copy).

There are numerous reasons people won't go ahead with a deal, but apart from the obvious objections such as the thing being sold is actually no use to the prospect or not what they wanted at all, value is usually what's missing.

Value beats price every time. It is for this reason that a great salesperson NEVER reveals the price until the buyer is ready to buy.

In other words, the price is only revealed when the deal is 99% done. Until a prospect is excited about owning an object and can clearly see themselves using it, the price will always be an issue. I've lost countless deals by revealing the price too early, so I make sure my copy covers every detail and possible objection long before the price is revealed.

There is one exception to this. Great copy should attract the right audience and repel the wrong audience. If stating the price early achieves this, then it's fine to do so. For example, selling the world's most expensive supercar tells us that price matters (the higher the better). There's a famous quote when a prospect looking for a Ferrari asked what the servicing costs were. The answer was "if you're asking a question like that, you can't afford the car."

NOTE: Always use the term COST when discussing the price of anything with a prospect. I've used the word PRICE in this section on purpose because that's how buyers perceive value before that value is explained in detail to them. Once they understand the value, they realise that the price is what it costs. It's an important psychological tool to remember in all negotiations.

Here's an example. If I tell you a car is priced at £50,000. You'll know it's negotiable (a price has no value). But if I tell you a car costs £50,000, the perception is it's non-negotiable (the implication is that if you add up all the parts that make up that car, they will come to £50,000).

Obviously, ethics matters here, but as I've said many times, villains will be villains whatever I say. All I can do is show you the tools to help you become a better negotiator and copywriter.

Pre-emptive objection handling

The best way to handle any objection is pre-emptively. For example, if we take "I can't afford it" as the most likely objection to the first part of our copy, then we need to make the case beforehand that they CAN afford it.

That could even happen in the headline "At last, a washing machine everyone can afford." The lede will then be all about washing machine costs and how this one beats everything else on the market.

If the objection was that they couldn't afford it right now, then we need to ensure there is a way they CAN afford it right now (perhaps a loan including a loan holiday period). Whatever the objections are, by handling them before they enter our prospects' minds, we put them at ease, and 'at ease' is a great place to start any conversation (written or spoken). From there we can start to build anticipation, desire, and action more easily.

Appendix B - Search engine optimisation (SEO)

Writing copy for ads should never depend on search engine optimisation. All ads are there to sell, not to be optimised so they show up in search results. Why? Because any ad worth its weight will sell the product regardless of attempts to trick search engines into thinking it's worth ranking.

Here's another reason. If the copy in an ad is tweaked to get it higher in search engine results, then it will compromise itself in terms of persuading readers to buy. What is optimised for search, de-optimises for sales.

NOTE: I am referring here to sales landing pages not the copy for pay-per-click ads that send people to those landing pages - although the exact same thing applies to those too (optimising a paid ad for search rankings is pointless since that's what we're paying for - to have our ads ranked at the top). Ads still need to be optimised of course, but that's for improving their conversion rates, not for search engine ranking positions.

What about content?

You could say the same thing. Optimising for search, de-optimises for reading (and to be read is the primary purpose of any piece of writing).

It takes an expert writer to come up with top quality content that has also been optimised to fool search engines into thinking it's somehow better than the rest, but is it worth the effort? I doubt it. Google is far cleverer than most of us think (they have hundreds of PhD qualified engineers writing code using artificial intelligence to stop people from gaming the system - and the whole point of SEO is to do exactly that).

Does SEO matter at all?

The point of a good search engine is to link to the best possible articles that people are looking for. Anything optimised for a search engine is not optimised for the audience. You cannot optimise anything for two separate purposes.

In the past, people spent inordinate amounts of money having articles optimised for search engines. But it was always at the expense of their reputation. Things have moved on since those days, and search engines like Google use the most advanced algorithms to discover which articles answer users' search queries the best.

Link farms and other artificial SEO techniques were blacklisted long ago by the search engines. Even the simplest of SEO ideas such as using the name of the industry you work in as your domain name have zero effect on search engine results (Google made this knowledge public in 2020).

Keywords

One of the last bastions of SEO are keywords and meta tags (see Keywords and Meta tags in the glossary). Google dropped the keyword meta tag many years ago, and now, even the meta description tag is losing its once powerful position. According to research done in 2020, less than 30% of results in Google display the meta description tag text (instead, Google now picks out a relevant part of the content to display as a description).

Which leads us to the last point.

How long should content be for SEO?

Content should be as long as necessary to give a full answer to a search query. This is still ambiguous though. It depends on what is being searched for compared to what is currently being served up in search results.

If users spend more time on one page than another, we can assume that page must be more relevant, but is it? Not always. If a page is well written, it can happily go off at slight tangents and still hold the reader's attention (signalling to the search engine that the page was a good result to display - even though it may not be the best result).

This is why many people suggest content should be longer than 1500 words if you want it to rank on page 1. But in time, Google and other search engines will get wise to these tricks too.

Think about it like this. If someone wants to know what time it is in New York, the best answer is going to be a single word (e.g., "10pm"). If, on the other hand, they want to know the history of New York, the best answer will most likely contain many thousands of words (right now Wikipedia comes out on top with around 7000 words).

So it's all down to the query and context. If you want to maintain a great reputation, write your ads and your content for the intended audience and nothing else.

Appendix C - Features, advantages, and benefits (FAB)

Never forget your FABs when writing content. F is for features. Without features, we will be creating blind copy (see glossary for more information) because features are the ONLY way we and our prospects get to know what we're selling and how those features might benefit (the B in FAB) our prospects.

A feature is something concrete - a switch on a kettle, the number of pages in a book, the search facility on a website. Think about features as what products have, do, or are made of. Without knowing a product's features, we have no idea whether they're useful. But when we do know the features, we can start to reveal a thousand reasons (benefits) why someone might want to buy one.

For example, without the automatic off switch on a kettle, it could boil all the water away and eventually catch fire, even burning the whole house down. So the benefit of this is security and safety. The feature of having, say, 1000 pages in a book, tells us it's a big book, and if it's from an author we love, then the benefit is we're going to get more to read from our favourite author for our investment in buying the book.

So what is the A in FAB? A is for advantage. Almost every product has competitors, and one of the top things every competitor is trying to do is become first in their market. The only way to do that is to be better than every other competing product. We call these extra features and benefits Advantages. When writing copy, ask yourself what advantages each feature of a product has over its competitors. Whatever they are, assuming those features fix the main problem our audience needs solving, become the unique selling points (USPs) in our copy.

Appendix D - Rhetoric

A few thousand years ago, the Greeks created and categorised a way of speaking and writing, and called it: "The Rhetoric." It revolutionised the world and rhetoric is now the language of choice for almost everyone who holds a position of power (in particular politicians).

Most people think rhetoric consists of anything that sounds exaggerated or made up (or even plain simple lies), but it's so much more than that.

For example, without rhetoric, propaganda wouldn't exist. It relies on it. Rhetoric is not just a 'way with words' or the 'gift of the gab', it's a toolkit of persuasion techniques (in fact, it's a very large toolkit).

To find out how large, get yourself a copy of Richard Lanham's "A Handlist of Rhetorical Terms" and you'll see what I mean. But it covers more than the ones many of us use, such as Hyperbole.

At its heart are three cornerstones on how sentences and paragraphs can be strategized. These are:

1. Deliberative.
2. Judgmental.
3. Emotional.

1. Deliberative techniques are about presenting two sides to an argument. These are the pros and cons of whatever is being discussed (or marketed or promoted in some way).

If we want to present a choice to a reader, we can use the deliberative method to explain the two sides and allow our reader to make up their own mind. If we want the reader to pick one particular side, then we can use the deliberative method to push them towards that side by being economical with the truth (if we're villains), or showing them why the best one is best if we're heroes.

2. Judgmental is our verdict on whatever it is we are deliberating. We can just use the deliberative technique on its own, or we can follow it with the judgmental technique and attempt to influence a buyer's decision directly.

3. Emotional is how we implement our copy to encourage people to take action. For example, if we discover that our market works best when they feel excited about something, then we can ensure that our copy invokes excitement at every turn.

When you're next analysing a piece of copy (your own or someone else's), see if you can spot any of these elements, and if they're lacking in any way, experiment by adding some of these ideas to your copy to make it stronger.

And remember you can talk about this to your prospects if you think it will help position you as the expert (just ensure it's not overdone - people get bored fast and it's our job to detect and avoid that no matter what).

Appendix E - Email marketing

New copywriters can be forgiven for thinking email marketing is any different from any other type of marketing. It's no surprise that this happens because marketers make out that email marketing is somehow special. It isn't.

It's just another way of taking someone on a journey from interested to sold. The trick, if there is one, is to ensure a good mix of 'I', 'you', and 'your' (POV) in your copy - in other words, make it personal.

You'll already know, having read this book, that the best copy talks direct to the prospect, which is why email is no different. If your copy gets personal, your readers will get personal too. That's what we want.

The best emails are written in sequences that take prospects on a journey from introduction to action (think of each email as another touchpoint - bringing your prospects closer to you and a future sale).

Appendix F - Fear

Most marketers have heard of FOMO (the fear of missing out) but is that the only fear?

Fear is one of the four cornerstones of copy (along with hope, greed, and envy) we can use to increase conversion rates.

A word of warning though, use fear with care. It's one of the darker sides of copy and is regularly used to spread fake news and other lies by those untouched by human morals (e.g., what most of us would call villains).

Here's a list of the most important fears that can be used in copy to help people make up their minds that something may just be more important to them than they realised:

Fear of the irrational

Every phobia is a fear of the irrational. This is the easiest fear to invoke if you know what a person's fears are. For example, losing our jobs is irrational (unless we've been told the company is going to make people redundant or is about to close).

So if we were tasked with writing some copy to advertise a job with a global corporation who had been around for a long time, we could use that fear to suggest that by joining this company, they "wouldn't need to worry about finding another job ever again".

Another example would be writing copy for a self-help course (or sell a self-help book). If we know that a person lacks self-esteem, then it's easy to invoke fear about what that's like and therefore, how a course like this could "fix it forever - order today and never worry about self-esteem again".

Irrational fears are fears that are about something that is unlikely to happen. If someone is worried about death, that sounds perfectly rational, yet we're all going to die anyway, so worrying about it is pointless (that's what makes it irrational).

Worrying about what would happen to our loved ones should we die is equally as irrational (because we have no idea when we will die or how that will affect our loved ones anyway), yet that single fear is strong enough to sustain an industry worth over $8 trillion in 2018 (and no doubt considerably more today). That industry is called life insurance.

Whatever industry, niche, product, or service you're writing copy for, think about the irrational fears people may have that are connected with it and how you might use those fears to strengthen your copy.

Fear of loss

Everything we possess that has some value to us is automatically attached to our natural fear of loss. This includes relationships, health, wealth, as well as our possessions. The insurance industry relies on the fear of loss to sell its policies (loss of life, loss of home, loss of transport, loss of medical care, and a whole lot more).

Fear of missing out (FOMO)

This is the one most marketers and copywriters know about and use regularly. Every countdown timer you see online is an example of the fear of missing out. The reason this 'persuader' is so well known is because it works.

Use the SURE framework to take FOMO to the limit. SURE is the acronym I came up with for the four words: scarcity, urgency, rarity, and exclusivity.

The countdown timer example is a concrete example of urgency in action. Scarcity and rarity can also be used effectively in terms of how hard something is to find, or how limited the supply is (e.g., "Only 4 in stock" - Amazon and other retailers use this everywhere).

You can also blend exclusivity into the FOMO mindset by strongly implying the prospect will miss out by, say, not being a member of some exclusive club "where other members enjoy things only the elite get to experience."

Fear of regret

It's been said many times that the one thing people on their deathbeds have in common is a regret that they did not do more with their lives. Even reading the previous sentence can show the power of regret: "Do you wish you'd done more? Well now's the time to step up your game and become the best copywriter on the planet." That's how to use regret to get people to take action.

Fear of rejection

Perhaps the loneliest feeling we can ever get is when we're rejected. The one thing most of us crave is love or acceptance from our fellow human beings, so any kind of rejection is bound to hurt, but if there's one thing that hurts more, it's not the rejection itself, but the fear of rejection.

Making someone feel special in your copy (and implying that they will soon be "part of the gang") is how you can use the fear of rejection to get someone to take action.

Fear is a dangerous tool, use it with care.

Appendix G - Triggers

A trigger is something that gets us to do something. Most of us are triggered by habit - e.g., when many of us get up in the morning, one of the first things we do is brush our teeth. The trigger that got us to brush our teeth was the very act of getting up.

For others it may be that eating breakfast triggers them to think about brushing their teeth (or anything else). But whether it's getting up, eating breakfast, or a myriad of other triggers that remind us to do certain things, it's the idea of cause and effect that we're talking about here.

Successfully forming new habits then, centres on finding triggers we can use to start taking the actions we need to take to get things done. This is also how we remove procrastination from our lives. For example, if you make it a habit to start writing directly after you eat breakfast, you'll never worry about writer procrastination again.

But this book is about copywriting, and that means persuading other people to do the things we want them to do, so it becomes obvious that if we can use triggers on ourselves to make things happen, then we can apply them to others too.

At the heart of all triggers is emotion (this is why it's one of the cornerstones of rhetoric). Emotion usually starts with some physical activity. We can force a smile on our face, which will result in a happy feeling, or we can witness some injustice, which might cause the emotional response of anger.

The emotional response itself is the result of a chemical reaction in our bodies, and it's that reaction that then causes us to do something (even if it's only to think or talk).

So as explained, a trigger represents the initial cause of a cause and effect system (i.e., a series of events). If we take a typical example of an advert for, say, sunglasses, we might start by talking about long summer days and the sun glaring in our eyes. This triggers a virtual physical response, and sets in place a series of thoughts on how we might prevent that.

Using frameworks such as PAS (Problem > Agitation > Solution - see the glossary) we can embellish the agitation the sun can cause, and introduce the obvious solution - sunglasses.

Start looking for triggers in every piece of copy you read. You'll recognise good copy because it will always contain some kind of trigger.

One thing to beware of though, is not to overdo them. If you trigger a series of events that get people to do something, don't then introduce another trigger to distract them into doing something else.

Appendix H - First principles (or how to get unstuck)

When we're stuck we have no idea what to do (that's the definition of being stuck). Yet we know there are numerous things we can do including seeking help. So why do we get stuck in the first place?

Here's a better question. Would you like a boiler plate method to get unstuck (or how about a method to never get stuck in the first place)?

And to go one step further, what about a method to get your prospective clients unstuck too (and get them drooling over every word you say)?

If you replied yes, then I have succeeded in doing just that (i.e., I got you interested and hopeful that you too will never be stuck again).

The problem with being stuck is the word stuck itself. It is infinite. When you're stuck you're stuck. It removes hope.

One solution is to reverse it by thinking about what it means to be unstuck, but that's not particularly helpful either (it's like being told "get over it").

This brings us to our secret weapon: first principles (and how to use it).

The method of first principles starts by getting us to look deeper into whatever it is we want to understand. So we start by asking the question "what is stuck?" And one thought springs to mind immediately. Being stuck is a PROBLEM.

From this one observation, I become unstuck. Why? Because by REFRAMING stuck as a problem, I arrive at this: EVERY problem has a SOLUTION. I can now move forward because my focus is no longer on being stuck, but on FINDING a solution.

NOTE: You might be objecting to the premise that "every problem has a solution." To that I'd say "every problem that does not have a solution is not a problem we are interested in." So how do we know what is and what is not a problem we are interested in? Rationalise it. Has anyone ever found a solution for the problem you need a solution for? (e.g., the problem of learning copywriting, the problem of finding clients, or the problem of helping clients grow their businesses?).

If the answer is YES (which it is), then that's a problem with a solution. On the other hand if we decided our problem was "how do I travel into the future?", then we ask the same question, and the answer is "we have no idea." Problems like that are NOT relevant to our task in hand - becoming a professional copywriter, finding enough clients to make a profitable business, and living the lifestyle we want to live is what we're after.

If it helps, reframe the premise like this: "Every RATIONAL problem has a solution." If you still find yourself stuck, ask yourself why (asking that question is another example of first principles thinking - there is always a way to an answer to anything, and that is to start by asking questions).

NOTE: If you read between the lines of the previous paragraph, you'll see I'm using first principles to answer the objection.

If we use the same framework to define the idea of first principles, the question becomes: what is first principles? – and the answer to that question is: a framework that gets to the heart of any problem so we can find a solution.

Every time we create a solution, we may also create another problem, but we will never be stuck anymore because we know that everything can be reframed using first principles thinking (which actually means asking simple questions such as: what is it?).

Every answer provides us with a new premise and every premise becomes the tool we can use to reframe our world and show us the next step.

This is all rather metaphysical, so let's get practical.

As you may recall in chapter 11, in the film Glengarry Glen Ross, Alec Baldwin told his assembled minions to: "always be closing" (or ABC). The offer to the most successful closer was a brand new Cadillac Eldorado (second prize was a set of steak knives - just to make the point that only one prize was worth winning).

It's important to understand that the offer of a Cadillac was not the solution (just the motivation to find the solution). The path to the solution was to discover the meaning behind ABC.

So the guys in the film knew there was a solution (ABC), they just had no idea how to implement it. They were no better off despite gaining the knowledge (as they went on to prove in the film).

But we know better because we know about first principles and can apply it to their problem. The idea of first principles is closely related to philosophy, which will help you implement the method every time you feel stuck (for more information on philosophy see Appendix K).

The first pillar of philosophy is called metaphysics. It's about the question of existence or what is real, to which the first step is to ask: what is it? That's how I figured out that first question: what is stuck? By asking it, I arrived at the answer: stuck is a problem.

Apply it here, and we get: what is ABC? I've now created a new problem so we ask the next question, which I'll do by way of allegory (allegory means story, and is another example of a rhetorical tool - see Appendix D - Rhetoric).

In The Wolf of Wall Street, Leonardo DiCaprio proves why he is king of sales by selling a pen. It's called the pen test. It doesn't mean very much, but it sure is fun.

All I have to do to sell someone a pen is amplify the value of the pen to such a degree as to make any future without the pen seem unthinkable.

To do that, we start with the first principles first step by asking: what is a pen? My solution then is to write down a list of everything I can think of about what a pen is (by the way, if I can't write at least 10 statements about a pen, it's easy to figure out that I'm not cut out to be a pen salesperson. From there I can also create a new premise: know your product or you'll never sell it).

Here's the next question: why is a pen useful? From there we arrive at the next: how do I know?

The "how do I know?" question is crucial. It came from the second pillar of philosophy – Epistemology (also known as the study of knowledge - or "how do I know?"). For example, how do you KNOW you're stuck anyway?

The character played by Leonardo DiCaprio is on a mission to get his employees to make as much money as possible. He explains that they need to understand what they're selling and why that matters to their prospects.

He gives them the keys to their fortune by answering every question they have by way of allegory. This appendix has been about first principles, what that means, and how to use them, for example, to get unstuck.

And the simple answer is always the same - we start by asking questions. When enough questions are asked, we come to a conclusion. Whatever that conclusion is, is the answer we were seeking. Apply this every time you feel stuck, and eventually it will become a habit so ingrained, you'll never feel stuck again.

First principle thinking reveals the problems we are facing - and by implication, the problems our clients are facing too. It then reveals the answers and creates premises that allow us to move ahead, get things done, and create the businesses we want.

Appendix I - Neutralise gender

I've spent much of my life de-gendering everything. At first it was incredibly hard. There are so many times we feel we want to use pronouns such as "he" or "she", then guilt sets in as we start to feel we're using "he" too many times (mostly because of stereotyping via our education and upbringing). So we start mixing it up with "she" to lessen the shame, and then some pedantic old scholar comes along and tells us to "tell it like it is" and "to hell with political correctness", and then on the news there's a report of a woman being stoned to death for no good reason, and we remember why the stereotyping of gender is bad.

So I started forcing myself to use the pronouns "they", "their", and "them" whenever it felt like a he or she was needed. And very slowly, it worked.

As I write this final section of the book I did a quick 'he/she' search of the text and there are 22 occurrences of he and 15 of she. In every case, it's because I'm referencing a REAL person. That is the ONLY time you'll ever find me using those pronouns, and that's because it's the only time it makes sense to do so.

As a result, I no longer worry about having to check for genderisation. I automatically use non-gender pronouns. As far as I - and my writing - are concerned, anyone can be anyone. Stereotyping is a thing of the past and something I wouldn't want to be associated with. I don't celebrate men or women, I celebrate us.

If you like the idea of this, then every time you feel the need (or confusion) to use a "he" or "she", force yourself to use "they", "their", or "them" instead. That may mean editing the sentence so it still flows and doesn't sound or feel awkward, but you will get there, and you'll find people loving you for it without even knowing why.

Appendix J - USP

A unique selling point or proposition (USP) is how you position yourself, a product, or a company to your market to let them know a) you exist, b) you're different, and c) why they should buy whatever you're selling right now.

But searching for a USP when one doesn't exist can be a little daunting. For example, if you're a general copywriter (i.e., you don't specialise in any particular niche), then you're amongst a large group of more or less identical looking people as far as your target market is concerned.

So how do you stand out and be noticed? One way is to brand yourself. You could do this simply by wearing a brightly coloured hat wherever you go (there are numerous professional speakers and a few pop stars who do this successfully).

It doesn't have to be a hat though; you could wear any type of clothing as long as it stood out (lots of celebrities from all walks of life choose this – British comedian Harry Hill did it with his oversized giant shirt collars).

What has any of that got to do with copywriting? Nothing. It's just a way to be SEEN to be different (and for those willing to try it, it just might be the one thing you're missing).

The problem is there are a million look-alike products and companies out there plying for trade (not just us copywriters). So what makes them different? It's often a combination of a few things from the personality of their salespeople to regular special offers to constantly reaching out to prospects (the latter being the sure fire way to get business).

Let's look at an old favourite of mine – US brewer Anheuser Busch. They make beer along with hundreds of thousands of other brewing companies. They're all in the same boat. I mean, a beer is a beer right? WRONG. Of course not. It's a bird, it's a horse, it's a 1950s pinup girl (or was in our politically incorrect world back then).

So here's ten of the ways Anheuser overcame their 'commodity' problem (which you may be able to use yourself with a little tweaking):

1. Use your logo and a slogan to tell a story. They added an Eagle to their logo making it the Eagle of Beers (they did it again later with another of their brands: Budweiser – The King of Beers).

2. Be first by creating a geographically unique market out of thin air: "First National Beer Brewed Exclusively in Hell, Michigan" (I made that one up, but you get the idea).

3. Gender stereotyping (but see Appendix I - Neutralise gender). The 'Budweiser Girl' poster campaign lasted 30 years (advertisers still use the female and male form to sell things today including the old reliables of perfumes and cars, but just because some people think it's a good idea doesn't mean it's a good idea, there are many creative ways to win hearts and minds without reducing people to objects).

4. Launch a campaign. Anheuser's USP in 1914 was its year-long newspaper campaign against the threat to personal freedom from prohibition. When prohibition came, they embraced it and created a new alcohol-free product called Bevo (first to market USP). Half the brewers went bust during prohibition, but not Anheuser.

5. In the 1930's they used heavy horses to show their historical connection with brewing ("you may love your new car, but you can always rely on a traditional brew" – selling old as new).

6. In the 1950's they used their 100th anniversary to differentiate. And they attached further differentiation using the association of famous historical characters with their "The Beer of Your Lifetime Too" campaign.

7. By 1960 they'd become number one by associating their brand with the mass market. The "people like us drink beer like this" concept, or as they put it "Where there's life, there's Bud."

8. In 1965 they introduced 'value' as a USP with the simple slogan "It's worth it" (can you see how easy it is to create USP's? – just add a copywriter). They missed a trick

though. They made it about the beer, not the drinker. L'Oréal took the idea 7 years later and made it personal ("Because You're worth it").

9. Give it a nickname. Hey, why not use a nickname as your USP? And let's make it all warm and cosy "Meet Mr Copypuppy."

10. You can even USP on sound, as in the famous fizzy "Buscsssssshhhhh" sound of the cap popping off campaign in the 1970's. Schweppes did the same thing in the UK.

But what are people using today to mark them out as different?

Here's one that came up on my email feed. It's a pet insurance company named: "Bought By Many." My only question is: who in their right mind would name their company that?

Well, the founders did obviously, and they now claim to be the "Most trusted pet insurance provider in the UK" (their claim is backed up with a whole bunch of industry awards including Which? Magazine recognition, the Moneywise Customer Service Award and a Feefo Platinum rating).

So would you rename your copywriting business "Used By The Best" or "Beat This." Why not? I haven't seen this used before in the copywriting industry. Maybe we're all missing something.

Bought By Many run online pay-per-click (PPC) campaigns as part of their lead generation strategy (including advertising directly in people's email accounts via Google). They have around 170 staff.

Are they successful? Founded in 2011, they only moved into pet insurance in 2017, but they did it with 100% focus. The goal was market domination.

They got a large injection of cash from a venture fund in the Summer of 2020 – which is amazing considering they lost £8m in 2018/19 and £15m in 2019/20 (thus proving that success is not always to do with profit).

In their case, success is about market control (which they have). So how much of this success is down to their name? We don't know. They simply chose to be different, but they had a clear plan, went for it, and won (read their investor information and you'll see what I mean).

Without a USP we have no big idea (or anything much else). Even if we are geniuses or have genius products, we'll still be perceived as run of the mill mediocre. And if we write for clients and they have no USP (or none we can find), they'll be perceived as mediocre too.

This is no position anyone wants to be in, so finding a USP becomes a priority.

Here's another recent example. In my FB news feed, a sponsored video popped up. The video was of a 40+ year old guy teaching in front of a blue coloured whiteboard (the blue colour seemed a bit odd – maybe that was what got my attention).

The headline was awkward (I can't recall it, and even after looking at the screenshot later, it's still almost impossible to retain the words). Here it is: "Why 'New Targeting' is NOT how we scale Facebook Ads and the myth of...."

But I still watched the whole video from beginning to end (I don't do that very often – even in the interests of science – after all, if a video is boring to me – and I'm part of the target audience, I'm not going to learn much).

The big idea (i.e., the USP) was simple: "If you think targeting is the key for successful Facebook ads, you're wrong." This big idea has been used a hundred times – not that specific example, but the concept of debunking myths (and it doesn't even matter if the myth turns out to have been true all along).

It's the controversy that matters, which makes controversy another USP in your arsenal of big ideas. It's also another 'goto' that journalists look for. News anchors regularly interview pairs of people with opposite opinions just to get viewers to pay attention and stay.

In the example video ad I watched, they knew one thing – that any professional watching would know this was click baity, so they had to debunk that fast – and they did (or else I would have stopped watching within a few seconds).

They did this in a number of ways, but top of the list was telling us what we already knew to be true, which in this case was that the average click through rate of a Facebook (FB) ad was 1%.

Then they hit us with their claim. Their click rate was between 5% and 15% and ads didn't burn out in a week. Any FB ad professional knows a claim like that is phenomenal. I was hooked.

But here's the best bit. I am their target audience. I clicked the ad. I watched it till the end. I signed up for their webinar, and I bought their product ($1495). That is proof in itself (to me – the target audience) that they know something about FB ads. It's also proof to FB that this particular ad was worthy of a high quality score, which lowers the cost to the advertiser.

If you're stuck for a USP (for you or to help a client), think about any of the suggestions used here. There are a million ways to position things as outstanding if you use a little imagination.

Appendix K - The five pillars of philosophy

The most written about topic since we first learned to write is philosophy: the search for the meaning of life, the universe and everything. It's also tightly bound to a successful career in business, not least of which includes the copywriting industry.

There's no way anyone could ever read it all, but luckily for you, I've broken the entire subject down to five easy to understand pillars.

Learn these five pillars and you'll be able to create your own philosophy. It matters because it's only people who have a philosophy of life who get to understand what they're here for (which means they're amongst the very few who become the cause of change instead of the effect of change).

Before we go into the five pillars, here's a little something.

The quick buck

There is only one purpose to life: survival. There are only two positive ways to get there: create and nurture.

To convince yourself of this, just look around. Positive things happen when we create and nurture. Negative things happen when we don't - we cannot survive if we destroy everything (which is why all dictatorships eventually fail).

Quick buck products are created by people who ignore this principle (they're called quick because they don't last).

If you're in this for the long haul, you'll need this mindset (create and nurture) to survive.

Pillar One - Metaphysics

The first pillar of philosophy is perhaps the most important. It's called metaphysics (but don't let that put you off). It's the study of existence or "what is it?" Another question behind metaphysics is this: "Is it real - does it exist?"

Every myth, legend and delusional state comes from getting the wrong answer to this question.

The second our imaginations came into being, the world became mythical. Confusion, chaos and destruction reign when we get the wrong answer to this question. Propaganda is one example of it (boosted by rhetoric to increase its power).

As a copywriter of any sort, understanding this first pillar is at the heart of why people do what they do.

Whenever you're confused by something, first check that it really exists and is not some myth or propaganda.

Pillar Two - Epistemology

The second pillar of philosophy is called epistemology. It asks the question: "How do we know?"

When someone presents something as fact, unless you follow up with this question, you will never know the truth. We use this pillar to find the answer posed in pillar one: "Is it real?"

Epistemology is therefore the study of knowledge - how do we know what we know. It's also your best weapon in any negotiation. You can ask it outright (very challenging), or you can ask it quietly to yourself.

This second pillar not only uncovers other people's truths, it uncovers your own (but only if you're open to being truthful to yourself - which takes us neatly to the third pillar).

Pillar Three - Ethics

The third pillar of philosophy is ethics. It is the hardest of the five pillars to get. Even though we think it's about values, Ethics is really the Study of Action.

Like every pillar, it can be summed up in a single question: "How far are you prepared to go to get what you want?"

Whatever values we think we have, and whatever high ground we decide to take in the moment, our moral compass can swing in an instant if we, or someone we love, becomes threatened.

Or, and nearly as common statistically, if an opportunity appears that is just too much for us to ignore, our ethics and values can fly out of the window.

Ethics is the single biggest problem in business because we can and are manipulated by words - what we say and what we hear, what we write and what we read.

Whenever you get stuck and need to make a decision, remember that one phrase: "How far are you prepared to go to get what you want?" Your integrity and future reputation depend on it.

But don't worry too much because the fourth pillar exists to hold us to account.

Pillar Four - Politics

The fourth pillar of philosophy is called politics. Politics is the study of force. Politics is what stops us from doing what we want (and sometimes for very good reasons obviously). The question that sums it up is: "what's stopping me?"

It doesn't matter how much we hate politicians, we can't live without them because they represent and control harmful forces. That is, they're here to protect us from harm (including harming ourselves).

Pillar Five - Aesthetics

The fifth and final pillar of philosophy is called aesthetics. You may think aesthetics is about how things look, but aesthetics is entirely driven by the need for change (the need for new).

This is why aesthetics is also known as the study of change. The single question that describes it is this: "what is possible?"

Bearing in mind the third and fourth pillars of philosophy: ethics and politics, you can see how absolutely vital aesthetics is to the world - without aesthetics, nothing would happen.

Aesthetics allowed the character of Robin Williams in the film Dead Poets Society to stand on a table and get his students to see the world in a new way. Change the aesthetic and you can change the world.

14 Glossary

This glossary does not replace a dictionary (nor does it pretend to be one). It does not contain every term used in marketing (not by a long way), nor does it contain every term used in the copywriting industry (both would fill a book on their own). Instead, it contains what I hope are some useful terms and ideas to help those new to the industry.

4

4Ps: The four Ps of marketing: product, price, place, promotion. This can be expanded, and has been by many people (to a seemingly infinite number of P's), so here are a few more worth knowing: people, packaging, proof, and process.

There are countless ways of using this, but all that matters is to know that each 'P' word forms part of the playing field we operate on. That is, we need to figure out what the product is, its price, its place in the market, how to promote it, and with that, then understand that all these elements connect together to play their part in our businesses (it's also how systems thinking works - there are no separate parts, every part affects one or more other parts, which means that tweaks on individual parts without looking at the system as a whole carries a very real risk of damage to the system).

There are a couple of benefits I see from memorizing lists such as the four Ps, the first is to help us remember that systems consist of many parts, and the four Ps are a reminder of what most marketing systems consist of. The second is that it can come in useful when talking with prospects to help you position yourself as the expert.

A

Above the fold: Most newspapers are folded in two before they're sold (because it takes up less room). That means people only see the top half of the newspaper on a newsstand. This is why the name for that part of a newspaper (and indeed anything that is seen first) is called 'above the fold'. In the case of a website for example, it's the part of the page you see first on screen (i.e., before scrolling down to read more). Anything 'above the fold' is deemed premium content space, so it tends to cost more to have an advertisement placed in the top half of a newspaper or magazine page just as it does on a website (especially if it's the home page - which often has the most traffic).

Advantage: This term is part of the FAB persuasion framework, that is, explaining what some product does (its features), why that is useful (its benefits) and why it's unique (its advantage). See FAB and USP.

Advertorial: A style of ad composed to look similar to the content of the magazine or newspaper they were written for. They generally are educational or informative in nature with a call to action often made subtle in order not to put the reader off before they've got enough value from the copy. Advertorials are also used heavily in in-store video sales promotions and presentations where selling is the thing and the call to action uses every tactic it can to encourage sales - e.g., with buy one get one free style offers.

Affiliate: Any person or company who resells other people's products or services on commission. Affiliates are the prime drivers of the Internet Marketing Industry.

AIDA: Attention, interest, desire, and action. Perhaps the best known acronym (along with the four Ps) in marketing and in particular, copywriting. The idea being that nothing happens without first getting attention. Once someone's attention has been gained, it needs to be kept using interest, then built on further by increasing desire to the point where action is taken.

Alliteration: A rhetorical tool and figure of speech used in copy that consists of two or more words following each other that start with the same letter and used to make the text flow more easily (e.g., "Ten top tips...."). Be careful with this as overuse can have the opposite effect by sounding contrived (and therefore unbelievable, so losing trust).

Anchoring: Our minds are susceptible to suggestions, which means if we suggest anything at all to people, they find it impossible to not hear that suggestion. And that means they are forced to process it in their minds. So if we tell people that such and such costs £XYZ, then from that point on, that price has been 'Anchored' as £XYZ in their minds. If we then follow that up with something like "but today you can get £XYZ for half price", we have effectively added value to whatever it is we're selling. Anchors can be based on anything (not just price). Read more about anchoring including examples in chapter 8.

Angle: A way to make any piece of copy stand out from the crowd. The best angles say something that competitive pieces of copy don't. See also Advantage, Big idea and Hook.

Assets: Anything of value used in a campaign rather than being sold as part of a campaign (e.g., graphic design, copy, landing pages, funnels, billboard posters). See Collateral.

Authentic (authenticity): A lot is said about being authentic, but authenticity is not something we learn, in fact, it's the opposite. To be authentic is to be you exactly who you are. To be anything different would be fakery. So when you read opinions that tell you to (somehow) be authentic, all they really mean (or should mean) is be yourself. When it comes to copy though, the message should be this: Be Different. In other words it has nothing to do with being authentic (because you cannot BE authentic, you can only BE you). This is where the Big Idea makes far more sense. If you train yourself to get bigger ideas, your copy will become more unique, and that will help whatever you're selling stand out (and hopefully be more "authentic" than the competition).

Autoresponder: Any solution that automatically sends broadcast messages to groups of people via email. They are usually set up using opt in forms on squeeze or landing pages to add people to segmented lists, who are then sent sequences of messages to encourage them to take some kind of action. They are also used to send newsletters or other manual broadcasts to lists.

Avatar: A stereotypical description of a group of people as though they were one person (think of an avatar as the average of a group of people - e.g., if the group's ages ranged from 40 to 50, then the avatar would be aged around 45). Avatars help ensure copy aimed at a particular niche, segment, or market, remain focused on that particular market. See also Persona.

Awareness levels: An idea created by Eugene Schwartz in his 1966 book Breakthrough Advertising. Its premise is that every buyer is in one of 5 awareness levels in the context of interest in any particular product, and that once known, it becomes easier to write copy to attract, engage, and convert that prospect into a buyer providing they also have at least a small amount of desire for it.

B

B2B: Business to business. Almost all copywriters write for other businesses, so we are usually categorised as being in the B2B space. However, the copy we write for those businesses may be B2B or B2C (see B2C). There are two benefits in knowing this. The first is the effect it has on our awareness of the markets we're writing for (if we know we're writing to a consumer market, we may well adopt a different stance than when writing to business owners). The second is if we make a deliberate choice of client selection. For example, if we decide to target only B2B businesses, then it may well differentiate ourselves from our competition if we position ourselves as specialist B2B copywriters.

B2C: Business to consumer. By far the most commerce is done from business to consumer. It's where the majority of copywriting work is to be found. It's how economies work too. Any business that sells products meant for the general public is categorized as a B2C business. Any business that sells products that are sold to and used by other businesses are classified as B2B businesses (see B2B).

Back end: The infrastructure and process necessary to make further sales to the same audience after they've first bought something (see Front end). The idea is that the initial sale leads into further up, down, and cross sales in order to maximise revenue as quickly as possible from buyers.

Backlinks: Any link on the internet that points to another site is a backlink to that other site. Backlinks are said to be important to SEO as it implies that a site is popular with other sites. The problem is, backlinks have been heavily abused for decades, with a result that search engines do not value them as much as they used to. See Link farms.

Banner ads: Any horizontally shaped advert or advert space.

Below the fold: Below the fold is the area that is usually not seen first, and typically refers to the lower half of any newspaper page or the lower portion of any page on a website (e.g., if you need to scroll down to see more, everything revealed when you scroll down is known as below the fold). See also Above the fold.

Benefit: A benefit is how something will affect someone. Every feature should have at least one benefit. For example, the main feature of a pen is to write, but its benefit might be to sign a contract worth millions (see FAB).

Big idea: A big idea changes ordinary copy into something special. A big idea can be anything that makes something stand out from its competitors, but usually it's in the form of a unique selling point (see USP).

For example, a well known internet marketer once ran a seminar called The Big Idea. It had a four figure ticket price and sold out. The big idea was the big idea itself. The promise of the seminar was how to create and exploit big ideas to make big bucks.

Bio: Abbreviation for biography often used to describe the copy used on an 'About us' or 'About the author' page on a website, book, or other asset used to position a person.

Blind copy: Any copy that contains benefits without stating features. The idea is that without explaining what the product, service, or offer really is, the prospect will become so overwhelmed with the desire to purchase whatever it is being sold, they will do it 'blindly' (i.e., no matter what).

Blind envelope: A plain envelope not marked with a logo or any other identifying marks. Often used in direct response marketing to get people to open marketing letters by not making it obvious who the letter is from or what the contents are about.

Body copy: The main text of any piece of writing (i.e., all the text that comes after the headline and lede, and before the close).

Bonuses: The staple of the internet marketing industry, but also used by every other industry as a way of adding value without reducing price. Bonuses are additional offerings that may include physical products, services, information, or extensions (e.g., extra time allowed on offers that are time related such as memberships and loans). Use with care and always ensure bonuses are aligned with the main offer.

Bounce rate: A term used in search engine optimisation (SEO). A bounce rate is how quickly someone lands on a page and then returns straight back to where they came from (usually as a result of clicking on a result in a search engine and finding it doesn't answer their query). The higher the bounce rate, the less likely search engines will show that page again in the results. That's the theory. The reality is often different as sometimes a page delivers exactly what the user wants in seconds, and their return to the search engine was to search for something else or look for alternatives. Bounce rates can be lowered by making a page more interesting to its readers and also by inviting them to click further relevant links from that landing page (so they stay there longer and explore more of the site).

Brief: An outline or summary of work to do or done. See Copy brief.

Bump offer: A way to add an upsell to any offer, usually done at the shopping cart stage in an online ordering process where the buyer only has to tick a box to have something extra added to their order.

Business reply card (BRC - or envelope - BRE): Used in direct response marketing to encourage and make it as easy as possible for prospects to respond to an offer. These are often sent postage paid to make it as easy as possible for the prospect to respond.

Buy one get one free (BOGOF): Commonly used retail sales tactic to boost sales volume by giving away a product if another product of the same type is bought. Also called a 'two for one' offer.

C

CAC: Customer acquisition cost. The cost of acquiring a new customer (see COA).

CAS: Customer acquisition system. Any system that implements and keeps track of leads (prospective customers) and their journey to becoming customers.

Channel: Any outlet or publishing platform used to circulate copy (e.g., Google, Facebook, Microsoft Ads, YouTube, autoresponders, solo ads, newspapers, etc.).

Churn rate: Churn is the number of customers who stop buying compared to the total number of customers for a specific period of time (can also be applied to subscribers, products, or anything sold on a subscription basis). For example, if a company at any one time has 100 customers, but they find that 50 of them disappear each month, then their churn rate is 50%.

Classified ads: Before the internet, any consumer wanting to sell items tended to place a few lines of text to advertise what they had for sale in their local newspaper. These became known as 'Classifieds' as they were broken down by category to make what you wanted easier to find. There are many websites that now offer the same service. The first and probably most famous is Craig's List.

Close (also known as The Close or Closing): Every deal starts with an opening (that may be in the form of an advertisement or some other marketing material, or just a conversation), but nothing happens until the deal is sealed, that is, a contract is signed or money is exchanged. The part of any negotiation that deals with that final aspect is called "Closing" or "The Close."

Closing loop: A closing loop is a sentence, paragraph, or short excerpt that closes an open loop. That is, something that gives the reader the answer to the open loop portion of a loop designed to get the reader to read more (see Loops).

COA: Cost of acquisition. The cost of acquiring something (usually a new customer). E.g., if it costs £100 in total ad spend to bring one new customer on board, then £100 is the COA.

Collateral: Collateral is all the marketing materials that go along with a campaign. This could include incentives, brochures, reply paid envelopes (see Business reply card), or anything else that adds value to a campaign (see Assets).

Comp: A mock-up of some asset used for marketing or sales purposes. Back in the early days of print, a person called a compositor laid out all the text for a newspaper or advertisement by hand. The term 'comp' was coined from that to mean first sight of what they had laid out (these were also sometimes referred to as 'proofs' or 'proof copies').

Continuity program: Any product or service sold with ongoing regular payments (e.g., monthly membership or software fees). This term is mostly associated with the internet marketing industry. In the normal business world, this is called a subscription model.

Control (also known as a control piece): The 'control' is a piece of copy that currently converts better than all other pieces of copy used to sell the same offer. If a competing piece of copy beats it, that becomes the new control (and the old control is discarded). Understanding and explaining what a control is, is a strong way to sell yourself in any negotiation for copywriting work. For example, when asked if you have any guarantees that your copy will work, you might respond with "I guarantee my copy will outperform your existing copy or it won't cost you a penny." (see also Split test).

Conversion rate: The rate at which any prospect moves from any one stage in a sales funnel to any other. E.g., the conversion rate for prospects who visit a website and then sign up for a newsletter is calculated by dividing the number of sign-ups by the number of visitors and then multiplying by 100 (e.g., if 20 people signup out of 250 visitors, then 20/250x100 = 8% conversion rate).

Cookies: A way to keep track of visitors online. Now regulated in most countries. See GDPR.

Copy: Any piece of writing written to sell something. In the context of the print industry (e.g., newspapers and magazines) content is also referred to as copy (which is why there's so much confusion over the term), but for the copywriting profession, it always means an ad or other piece of writing designed to persuade someone to do something - which is usually to purchase a product or service. Note that the term copy is used for single pieces of work and also multiple pieces of work (so use copy NOT copies). Also, it doesn't usually need an article (in the grammatical context) in front of it (i.e., it is not "a copy", just "copy" - e.g., "can you write copy?" - not "can you write a copy", determiners and pronouns, such as "the" or "your" are fine, e.g., "where's the copy?", or "where's your copy?").

Copy brief: An outline of the scope of work for a copywriting article or project (see also Brief).

CPC: Cost Per Click. Used in online ads, the cost per click is how much an advertising platform (e.g., Google, Bing, or Facebook) charge an advertiser every time someone clicks on their ads. This is one of the metrics used to determine if an online CPC based advertising campaign is profitable.

Cross sell: Any product offered after an initial sale that is related to the initial sale but not necessarily needed in order to complete the initial sale (e.g., "now you have the car, how about this yacht"?).

CTA: Call to action: A call to action is any sentence or paragraph that asks the reader to do something (e.g., "Buy Now", "Phone for the best deal", "Fill in your details to find out more" etc.). It's usually placed at the end of a piece of copy, although can be placed more than once anywhere in the copy depending on how aware the audience is.

Customer persona: See Avatar, Persona.

D

Decision maker: The person who makes the final decision in any deal. Whenever you're prospecting for clients, you're always looking for the decision maker (and not the gatekeeper - see Gatekeeper). If you try to sell to anyone who turns out not to be the decision maker, you'll very likely have to sell yourself all over again (assuming you're given a second chance). Don't let this put you off though. Talk politely to everyone you meet whether they turn out to be the CEO or the janitor - sometimes they're on personal terms (see Six degrees of separation).

Deliverable: Any asset or collateral to be included as part of an advertising campaign or other copywriting project. Deliverables will often be outlined in a brief (see Copy brief).

Demographic: Normally used to describe a person or group of people by analysing their traits and backgrounds - i.e., their social and economic status. These include race, gender, age, likes, dislikes, religion, wealth, education, social circles etc. The idea being that once defined, it becomes easier to write copy aimed at a group of people who share a common set of demographic data (see also Persona).

Dimensional: See Lumpy mail.

Direct response (also known as direct response marketing or advertising): Any sales copy sent directly to specific people and asking them for an immediate response of some sort (or advertisements that do the same thing). The most common forms of direct response marketing include direct mail and broadcast emails sent by autoresponders to lists of prospects.

Display ads (display network): Any (usually image based) ad that appears on a website that is NOT a search engine is called a display ad. These ads are controlled by a large number of platforms, including the largest of all, which is Google. Display ads are passive ads in that they're not necessarily shown as a direct result of a search, but more likely because the advertiser believes you (the prospect) like the site the ad is being displayed on and will therefore be more likely to spend longer on the site and eventually click the ad. See Search ads.

Double bind: A technique whereby someone feels forced to do something or answer something. Used extensively by sales reps to get appointments or agreements on possible next steps. "Are you free today or tomorrow?" is a typical example (even if the person never wants to speak to the rep, they're only given two options - both of which bind them into an agreement). A more friendly way (but still a double bind) is to ask "When will you be free?" Whether you choose to use double binds is down to you and depends on your view of the world and your ethics.

Double opt in: This is a way of verifying an email address when someone signs up online to receive a newsletter or other electronic message by email. With double opt in in place, people who sign up online are sent a confirmation email with a link in it, which once clicked, proves that they were the same person who made the request. This method has become more predominant since online privacy laws were strengthened in recent years (see GDPR).

Downsell: Any product offered after an initial sale which is a) related to the initial sale, and b) cheaper than the cost of the initial sale.

E

Editing: After learning to write effective copy, editing is the next most crucial skill any great copywriter needs. In fact, I don't think it's possible to become a great copywriter without also learning to become a great editor (see chapter 10).

Email: Requires no explanation other than to mention it is still the most widely used method of information distribution other than word of mouth. According to Statista, 306 billion were sent every day in 2020 and increasing.

Email newsletter: Email newsletters are often used to build lists of prospects as well as keep existing prospects and customers up to date with everything going in a business including the announcement of new offers.

Evergreen: A term used to describe any product that is always on offer or for sale (as opposed to products restricted by time or quantity). In the internet marketing industry, the opposite to this is a product launch, where a short window of time is given to force people to buy using fear techniques such as FOMO (see FOMO and Product launch).

Exclusivity: One of four ways to increase the likelihood of action in any call to action (CTA) described in the SURE framework (see SURE).

F

FAB: Features, advantages, and benefits. An advertisement that shows the benefits and advantages of its features will always do better than one that does not (people need to know why a product is useful to them - if gives them a reason to buy). See separate entries for each element of FAB, and also the entry in this glossary for USP.

Feature: Every product has one or more features. A feature is what a product does. For example, the main feature of a pen is to facilitate writing. Another feature of a pen is to store ink. See FAB, benefit, and advantage.

First to market: First to market means that this is the first time a particular product or service category has been offered for sale to a particular market. Any product that is first to market has the potential to corner that market and dominate it by being the market leader. Whether that happens or not depends on the size of the marketing budget, the interest within the market, and the virality of that interest. It is no guarantee of success though (even under the protection of patents).

Flywheel: The idea of building momentum by building more on top of whatever you have so it becomes harder to stop (or undo) what's already been done. When applied to marketing, it means attracting, engaging, and strengthening relationships on a continuous basis so they build over time and become harder to break, thus keeping more customers and enabling stronger growth.

FOMO: Fear Of Missing Out. A strong persuasion technique used in copy to force a sale. The FOMO methodology uses elements of scarcity, urgency, and rarity, along with benefits and emotions such as envy to induce a strong need to buy. (e.g., "everyone loves the xyz, make sure you don't miss out as we only have limited stocks available").

Front end: The infrastructure and process of making an initial sale either to a new customer or from the sale of a new product to an existing customer. See Back end.

Funnel: See Sales funnel, Front end, and Back end.

Futurescaping: Showing someone what's possible in the future. This is usually followed by copy that takes them back to their current situation and emphasizes how much better it would be to have the future just suggested. Used extensively to power copy as well as deal making.

G

Gatekeeper: Any person whose job is to ensure only the right people get through to a decision maker. As copywriters looking for work, it is our job to know how to convince gatekeepers that we ARE the right people and should be put through to the decision maker. This takes time and perseverance to discover and can only be done effectively through the experience of real sales calls - do this as often as you can if you want to become great at sales.

GDPR: General data protection regulation. Originally drawn up for the EU (European Union), GDPR (in various forms and different abbreviations) have been drawn up in most countries. Always check your local regulations (and the regulations of any countries you trade with) to ensure you stay within the law - especially when it comes to personal data, privacy, and cookies.

Goto person: In marketing, the 'goto' person is what we all try to become. We want the world to know that if they need the particular problem we fix to be fixed properly, then we are the person they need to go to above all others. This is why it's best to niche down and not be a general copywriter (because the world is full of general copywriters and doesn't need any more). See Niche and USP.

275

Guarantee: A guarantee is any promise backed up by compensation of some sort if the promise is not met. If whatever is being sold has a guarantee, it can help the conversion rate. For this reason, it makes sense to display guarantees prominently to help drive more sales. Generally, the bolder the guarantee, the higher the conversion rate.

H

Headline: The most prominent piece of text in any piece of copy, usually placed at the top, and highlighted in some way (e.g., by using a larger font, different colour, or different font to the body copy). The purpose of a headline is to get the reader to read the rest of the copy, therefore the best headlines grab the readers' attention and hold it long enough for them to want to read more.

Hook: A hook is a sentence or two of text to capture the attention of a reader to get them to want to find out more. A hook can be the headline (or part of the headline) or any piece of text placed early on in a piece of copy. See also Big idea and Angle.

Hyperbole: In advertising, a rhetorical device used to hype up whatever is being sold by making outrageous claims to the point of disbelief.

I

Inbound marketing: The idea of inbound marketing is that prospects or customers come to you rather than you go to them. It's another way to describe passive marketing in that you put up, say, a website in the hope that people will discover it and contact you. It's a bit of a myth though, since everything happens due to cause and effect, so it all has to start with you doing something (e.g., writing content and publishing it on a website). See Outbound marketing.

Internet marketing: also known as the Internet marketing industry IM or IMI. You may think that any business that advertises online is the internet marketing industry, and you wouldn't be wrong, but in the context of the label "Internet Marketing" and "Internet Marketing Industry", this is a special category that is made up of three core offerings: 1) information products, 2) memberships sites, and 3) certain software products. The most common membership sites revolve around coaching and the self-help industry. You can recognise IM style products by the way they are marketed through (mostly) outrageous claims, guarantees, and bonuses, along with massive affiliate partnership promotions (also known as Joint ventures or JVs), and time limited product launches. Copy written for the IM industry tends to take hyperbole to the limit compared with any other industry.

J

Johnson box: Any area of a page or piece of copy that stands out from the rest. Johnson boxes (also known as callouts) highlight something that may be exclusive or unusual and are there to call attention to themselves and keep readers interested.

Joint venture (JV): Any partnership between one or more parties. Although the idea of joint ventures has been used in the business world for millennia, it has taken on a whole new meaning in the internet marketing (IM) world (see Internet marketing). In the IM world, it usually refers to affiliate programs that often pay 50% or more of the selling price as commission to affiliates. In the bricks and mortar world of business, this could never happen since profit margins are directly defined by competition and costs are of paramount importance to the viability of those businesses. But since most IM products are electronic or virtual, the profit margin is often near 100%. This is why IM products are marketed so heavily with rhetoric and blind copy techniques with bonuses galore and guarantees designed to sell more volume regardless of the integrity or suitability of the goods being sold.

K

Keywords (or keyphrase): Any word or phrase that is commonly searched for online. Keywords are often embedded into online articles to increase their search engine ranking (i.e., to get them closer to the top of page 1, the idea being to get more visitors to a website). See Appendix B - SEO.

Kicker: A cliched term used to describe an element in a piece of copy that helps build desire (e.g., "And here's the kicker...[insert some amazing claim or benefit]").

Killer copy (also known as killer offer): Any copy that converts exceedingly well (i.e., far better than expected or average). See Control.

KLT: Know, like, and trust. This term is commonly used in networking circles where members are repeatedly told they will get more business if they become known, liked, and trusted by their peers. Whether that is true is hard to prove since many people buy goods and services from companies they don't know, or worse, hate. What matters is a good offer as explained in the pages of this very book. Having said that, if any of those three matter at all, focus on trust.

KPI: Key performance indicator. Think of a KPI as an outcome or goal. They are used to measure performance. For example, if we want to double our revenue this year, then we will set a KPI called "Double this year's revenue." At the end of the year we can compare our performance with our KPIs, and if any fail (or exceed) expectations, we can adjust them appropriately for the following year. KPIs can be set for any period of time (not just annually - it all depends on how often you want to check progress), what matters is they are concrete (must be measurable) and are time bound (they have a deadline). KPI's are often created in groups that represent different aspects of the operation of a business (for example, financial KPIs, production KPIs, development KPIs, etc.).

L

Landing page: A landing page is any online page that a prospect, customer, or visitor lands on after clicking an ad or some other link. In fact, every page on the internet is a landing page, but the term is mostly used in the advertising and internet marketing industry to describe a page used to sell something. A landing page is often part of a sequence of pages known as a sales funnel (see also Squeeze, Splash pages and Sales funnel).

Lead generation: The act of finding and recording the details of new prospective customers with a view to marketing to them.

Lead magnet: Anything that encourages a prospect to take action such as sign up to a subscriber list, usually at zero or low cost. Examples include eBooks, reports, cheat sheets, webinars, and sample merchandise.

Leads: People who may one day become customers. Also known as prospects (or prospective customers).

Lede: A variation of the word lead or leader, meaning the opening paragraph or two of any piece of copy. A lede expands on the promise of the headline and hooks prospects into reading more (see Big idea).

Legitimate interest: A way to get round privacy laws by claiming that permission was granted for contact to be made because there was an existing relationship. Always talk to a lawyer if in any doubt about privacy or cookie laws. Although most countries have their own laws, some of those apply globally.

Leverage: Any angle that gives you an advantage is called leverage. If you know something that a prospect doesn't know and that the prospect would be willing to pay for if they did know, gives you leverage over that prospect. A great example is a control piece (see Control piece).

Lift note: Any attachment to a piece of copy that encourages the reader to read more (or take action in some other way). Often attached as a post-it style note, they usually contain additional messaging (sometimes hidden under the note) and are there to get the reader's attention.

Link farms: Any group of websites that have been set up with the sole purpose of creating backlinks to other sites in order to boost those other sites' rankings in the search engines. This activity breaks most search engines' terms of service and usually results in heavy ranking penalties to the sites of all those involved in creating them.

List building: To build a list of prospects. Strongly associated with the internet marketing industry who actively grow large lists online and then sell (usually through affiliate programs) various products to people in those lists in return for a commission based on the sale price.

Loops: A loop is a literary device to attract and keep the attention of a reader. There are two parts to a loop. The first opens it with a sentence or two that compels us to want to find out more. The second closes it with the answer to whatever it was that compelled us to read on. The gap (or length of copy) between the open and closing loop segments can be any length, with the proviso that the longer the gap remains open, the more frustrated the reader will get - to the point where they may stop reading completely. The best loops keep readers excited and reading without frustration. Multiple loops can be started, each with different ending points (see Open and Closing loop).

Lumpy mail (also known as dimensional): Any asset supplied along with marketing materials to a prospect (often used as an incentive to get the prospect to open the envelope or packaging the offer arrives in). The idea is to deliver something that looks a little different to normal mail to get prospects to take notice - hence the terminology - 'lumpy' mail.

M

Marketing: Any activity associated with spreading the word about a product, service, brand, individual, or company. This includes the design, manufacture, and distribution of all materials used to sell whatever is being sold.

Marketing mix: Marketing involves many different methods, disciplines, and channels. The term 'marketing mix' refers to how many of these methods, disciplines, and channels are being used at the same time on a particular project, campaign, or simply the marketing of a business in general.

Market segment: A portion of a market. See Segment.

Masthead: A horizontal area or section at the top of a page (online or in print). Often used to state what something is about (e.g., the title of a newspaper or a website).

Message to market match (MMM): When a message aligns perfectly with a market, it is said to have a message to market match. All copy should be written with this in mind.

Meta tags: In the world of SEO, meta tags were once considered important. They were a way to briefly describe the contents of a page so it could be understood better by search engines. Unfortunately, they have been so abused by spammers (trying to get pages to rank higher) that they have become almost meaningless. Having said that, some meta tags are still used, and search engines like Google say they are still taken into account, albeit with less value attached.

Mockup: A way to show how something will look before it has been completed. Mockups are often made of advertisements to show what they could look like before any serious money has been spent on their production or distribution. Mockups are also often used to demonstrate prototype designs or products.

Mover: Anything that gets people to take action. Typical examples are hope, fear, and emotion.

MRR: Monthly recurring revenue. Any offer that involves some kind of monthly subscription will have an MRR rate. This is simply the amount of money being generated each month by that subscription.

Multi-level marketing (MLM): Best avoided. Think of MLM as affiliates on steroids, the main difference being that for normal affiliate schemes, the pyramid is (usually) 2 levels deep (the supplier or manufacturer being the top level where the bulk of the money ends up) and the seller level being the affiliate level where the rest of the money is distributed among the sellers). With MLM, there is (usually) an unlimited number of affiliate levels with those on the bottom rung earning almost nothing and often losing money because they're unable to sell what they were (often) coerced into buying in order to become a member of the MLM scheme in the first place.

Multidimensional marketing: A recent term meaning using every channel and means possible and simultaneously to market something (e.g., face-to-face, video, blog, tweet, podcast, etc.). See also Marketing mix.

N

Niche: Everything has a hierarchy. If we look at business, at the top is the word Business itself. After that comes a whole slew of industries (e.g., energy, food, housing, security, entertainment), and each of those can be further categorised into things like manufacturing, distribution, and retail etc. Whatever way you slice up business, every slice you make (e.g., the retail side of energy) has subsections within it. And furthermore, each subsection can also be sliced and so on. This 'slicing' from the top down is how niches are found. A niche is therefore a subsection of business, but what makes a niche valuable are the number of customers within that subsection, the level of competition, and your ability to create or deliver what that subsection most desires. The more you slice, the more unique that niche becomes in terms of those 3 main factors (customers, competition, and problems to be solved). Get it right and you'll find yourself the market leader of that niche. That's the goal for anyone starting out in any business.

Nixie (also known as undeliverable): Any mail or post that is undeliverable for any reason.

O

Objections: Objections, and overcoming them, is how we learn to write the best converting copy. An objection is any reason, no matter how trivial, that stops someone from buying something. In fact, the only reason anyone decides to walk away from a deal is because they object to some aspect of it. The most common reasons are to do with cost (e.g., "it's too expensive", or "I don't have the money right now"). But these are rarely the real reason. This is such an important topic to understand and handle, there's a whole section devoted to it in Appendix A.

Offer: Any copy that has an option to buy contains (or is) an offer. An offer is a combination of things that entice a reader to take action. For example, the most common offer of all is a product and buy button. A stronger offer might include a discount (or implied discount by using the word SALE). A complex offer may involve a number of conditions, all of which, when complied with, result in something that cannot be obtained elsewhere. If the benefits of a complex offer (or indeed any offer) matches exactly what a prospect wants, it will almost certainly result in a sale (and an increased conversion rate).

Open loop: An open loop is a sentence that compels us to want to find out more. A headline is an example of an open loop if it gets the reader to want to read more. The point of an open loop is to get and keep the reader's attention until it is closed. See Closed loop and Loops.

Open rate: The rate at which emails or other electronic messages are seen by its recipients. For example, if a newsletter is emailed to 100 people but only 10 of them open the email, the newsletter's open rate will be 10%.

Opt in rate: The rate at which visitors or prospects sign up to some offer (usually by submitting their email address in an opt in form). If 100 people visit a landing page with an opt in form, and 10 of them sign up, the opt in rate will be 10%. See Double opt in.

Outbound marketing: Every time you make contact with a prospect, you are putting marketing into practice.

Outbound marketing is just another name for proactively contacting people and letting them know what you do.

P

Packaging: All products that need to be packaged in any way, will benefit from the services of a copywriter to write the words for the packaging (if you're ever asked to write some copy for some packaged product, always suggest they also might like to hire you the next time they update the packaging - this will encourage repeat business).

PAS: Problem or pain, agitate, solution. This is a simple copywriting framework where you start by explaining the problem, then increase the intensity and consequences of what might happen if that problem is not solved quickly, and ending the copy with a solution to fix it. The idea being that by increasing the pain, the prospect will find it hard to resist buying the solution.

Passive ads: Passive ads refer to advertising that is being displayed NOT as a result of a direct search for whatever the ad is advertising, but more usually because the advertiser knows that the audience likes a particular location, so may see the ad in amongst the content on, say, their favourite site.

Passive income: Income received from a product that sells without needing any (or very little) management. Royalties from books and music are the two most common examples. Licencing of products and technology are another.

Persona: The attributes that make up a typical prospect in a market (such as their age, gender, likes, dislikes, etc.). See also Avatar.

Point of view (POV): All writing is written from a certain point of view. This can be in 1 of 3 states: first person POV, second person POV, or third person POV. first person uses pronouns such as I, me, we, or us. Second person POV uses pronouns such as you or yours, and third person POC uses pronouns such as they or them. POV is hugely important in all forms of writing.

Positioning: Everyone in the world has a 'position' on something. A 'position' is an opinion. To see how that works, ask yourself this: "what's your position on money?" or "what's your position on work?" In business, a company's position is how it sits in a particular market. For example, your position as a copywriter might be: "the world's best medical equipment sales copywriter." A position is how you want your market to see you (and how that position helps you stand out in that market). Note that however you try to position yourself (or a client or product) is ultimately down to the buying public whether that position is accepted.

Postscript (PS): Always use a PS at the end of your communications. Readers often scan down emails or letters to the end, so a PS can be used to entice them to go back to the top and read it all. Used in this context, a PS might say something like this: "PS. If you loved what I said in paragraph 3, then you'll also love what I'm going to send you tomorrow."

Presell: Any piece of copy that presells whatever is being sold. This may typically be a piece of copy in an early part of a sales funnel sequence. It might also be an ad or blog post that includes a call to action if someone wants to find out more. Presells are used to warm up cold (or less aware) audiences.

Press release: Any piece of copy sent to news agencies with news of a product, event, company, or any other type of announcement deemed worthy enough to get the attention of local, national, or international press. Note that the biggest failure of all press releases is to send anything that sounds like sales copy.

Product launches: Product launches exist in every area of business, but they have been made particularly famous by internet marketers using limited time techniques to coerce people into a quick buying decision. These types of product launches are usually associated with large affiliate and partner networks often paying 50% commissions in order to feed explosive, but usually short term, growth and profits.

Promise: A headline or lede without a promise will fail 99% of the time. A promise is a hint of what's to come, and with that, we build hope (or fear). Either way, the point of a promise is to get the reader further into the copy (in pursuit of some kind of answer). The bolder the promise the higher the interest - but also the higher the doubt, therefore bold promises should be supported by solid proof to gain trust.

Proof: Without proof or evidence of any claims made about a product (e.g., in a headline), doubt sets in. The longer the doubt remains, the bigger the objections become. At some point, unless fully handled, objections stop sales. Always ensure you gather enough proof to cover all objections. Not to be confused with 'proof copies' - see Comp.

Proof copies: See Comp.

Proofreading: Checking copy for errors (also known as typos) including spelling mistakes and grammar.

Prospects: People who one day may become customers. Also known as leads.

Psychographics: See also demographics. Every audience is different. Some may be identified, for example, by their job, others by their income, and yet others by their social status.

Q

Questions: Without questions, no research can be done. Remember the phrase "always be asking questions" (ABAQ). Remember also to listen deeply once a question has been asked. Lousy salespeople are lousy because they fail to ask questions and discover what problem needs to be solved, and when they do, they fail to listen properly to the answer.

R

Remarketing: A way to deliver ads online to people who have already shown an interest in something. There are two major benefits from retargeting advertising this way. The first is to ensure that ads are only seen by people who are interested. The second is to keep the advertising spend down by not wasting money on showing it to people who are not interested. This is also called retargeting.

Retargeting: See Remarketing.

Rhetoric: If there's a secret to successful copy, it's the use of rhetorical tools that help the copy achieve its purpose. See appendix D.

Risk reversal: The idea of risk reversal is to claim that all the risk for buying a product is taken by the seller - and not the buyer. This is rarely true, since at some point the buyer will have to part with their cash (and that in itself is the riskiest part of any deal). Therefore people who claim they take all the risk can only truly do so if they both supply the product for free AND make up for any time wasted if the product is rejected. This type of claim is most often used in copy written as part of a guarantee.

ROAS: Return on advertising spend. If we spend £100 on advertising and we get back £200, then our ROAS ratio is 2:1 (for every dollar we spend, we get back two dollars). ROAS is an important KPI in advertising.

ROI: Return on investment. Perhaps the most used acronym in business. If it costs £100 to sell a £200 product, the return on that investment of £100 would be 200% (net return on investment divided by investment multiplied by 100). Note that the example used here doesn't take into account any of the costs associated with acquiring or manufacturing the product or selling it other than the advertising costs. Always be careful to include every cost when working out the real return on any investment.

Run of paper (ROP) (or run of page): Any advert deemed ROP usually costs less as it means permission has been given for the newspaper to place it wherever it wants within the paper. This is also called "run of site" when referred to advertising online.

Run of site (ROS): See Run of paper.

S

Sales funnel: A sale can happen immediately, or it can take any number of steps. Any sale that takes more than one step is called a sales funnel. Typical examples are lead magnets to build subscriber lists, who are then taken to landing pages, and ultimately to a shopping cart.

Sales page: Any page that has sales copy on it. A sales funnel tends to consist of multiple sales pages, each one taking the reader closer to a buy button.

Search ads: Ads that are displayed in search engines are called search ads. They directly target people searching for specific information. These types of ads are called active ads as opposed to passive ads because the intent of the searcher directly relates to what the ad is advertising. See Passive ads.

Search engine optimisation (SEO): Using certain words and other techniques in copy and content to help influence search engines such as Google and Bing to rank those pages higher in the search results. See appendix B.

Segment: A section of any audience that shares similar demographics or interests. As a verb, it means to create individual sections (e.g., "now segment your audience by their interests, and email each segment according to what they have in common").

Sidebar: In the context of advertising, a sidebar is any extra column in a piece of sales copy (left or right) that is not obviously a part of the main column or body text. This is often used to add extra bullet points or other call outs to increase attention.

Six degrees of separation: It's often said there are only six degrees of separation between the lowest of the low and the highest of the high. For example, in terms of status within a company, if you know the janitor, that janitor will know someone next up in the hierarchy, and that person will know the next one up, and so on until by the sixth person, you'll probably discover a direct connection with the CEO or company president. Always remember this if you value your future allegiances no matter who you are talking with. Be kind to all you meet. See Decision maker.

Solo ads: A solo ad is ad space bought from a third party who has an email list they're willing to share with the advertiser. Mostly used in the internet marketing industry.

Splash page: Any page on a website whose purpose is to make an announcement of some kind. Often this is to some offer and includes a button or other link that takes them to a squeeze or other landing page. A typical splash page example will use a background graphic and have a minimal amount of text. It's there to get one thing done (as opposed to other landing pages that may include menus, links to blog posts, ads, and any other number of distractions). Splash pages may also feature a video if it makes sense to do so.

Split test (also known as split testing, A/B split test): Testing two or more versions of copy selling the same product to find out which version converts or performs better. The nearer the differences between those versions are to the top of the copy, the more obvious the results, however, testing different images, no matter where they are placed, can also bring about large improvements to conversion results. Without testing one piece of copy against another for the same product, a copywriter can never be certain if the copy could be improved (see Control).

Squeeze page: Any page on a website whose purpose is to get contact details from the visitor (usually their name and email). Most squeeze pages focus on one thing in order not to distract the visitor.

Story driven copy: Add a story to your copy to gain interest and you have 'story driven copy'. This is often used on less aware audiences who need an introduction to whatever is being sold so they can experience the benefits from a different point of view (often using a third party point of view to garner more trust).

Strapline: Any phrase or slogan (often a subheadline) attached to a brand, product or heading. See also Tagline.

Subheadings: Any heading other than the main heading. Subheadings help split copy up to make it less imposing and more readable. Often subheadings, when read on their own, tell a story about the copy (the idea being that people who like to skim read first, get the message).

SURE: Acronym for scarcity, urgency, rarity, and exclusivity, the main four incentives used to increase the likelihood of action in any call to action (CTA).

Swipe file: Any collection of copy put together so that people can read it in a single place. They might consist of best-selling headlines or best direct response sales letters. They can also be compiled from short copy ads (e.g., classified ads) or display ads.

Systems thinking (also known as systems theory): The idea that all parts of a system need to be taken into account in order to understand how something works (not just a single component of a system). Karl Ludwig von Bertalanffy's 1968 book General Systems Theory explains why thinking about a system in general terms rather than specifics is a better way to understand the world.

T

Tag: Tags help us analyse things. Think of tags as categories. If everything that needs categorising is given a tag (e.g., a hashtag on social media or a tag using Google Tag Manager) it helps us identify groups of items or groups of data.

Tagline: Any slogan that supports a brand name (or sometimes a headline). L'Oréal's "Because you're worth it" is a typical example, as is Nike's "Just Do It."

Target market. Any audience sales copy is aimed at. Without a target market or audience in mind, few ads will ever make enough sales to cover their costs (or make a profit).

Teaser: Anything added to a piece of copy to attract or engage a reader's attention (teasers are often used on the front of envelopes to get readers to open the envelope). A teaser can be a phrase or something physical such as a post-it note used to hide something or that claims something will happen if some kind of action is taken.

Testimonials: Testimonials are written, audio, or video proof that a product or service does what it says from people who have used or owned it.

Thud factor: The weight of a product and the effect of that weight on the subconscious mind of a prospective buyer (e.g., "if it weighs that much, then it must be good", or "if it's that heavy, then it must contain a lot of information"). Often used in images to sell 'information products' by making them look bigger or more substantial than they really are.

Traffic: Another word for visitors to a website.

Trigger: Anything that gets someone to do something starts with some kind of trigger. For example a call to action (CTA) is a trigger. Another example is any headline that gets the reader to want to read more. Triggers invoke a response, and since all responses come from an initial emotional change of state (including emotions that are triggered by external events that cause a change in one or more of our five senses) it makes sense to figure out which triggers work best for which situations. Read more about this in Appendix G - Triggers.

Touchpoint: Every time a prospect sees, hears, or even touches something to do with a product, service, or brand is called a touchpoint. Touchpoint theory says that the more touches someone gets with a particular product, service, or brand, the more likely they are to buy. We are often told that 7 touchpoints are needed, but whilst that may be true for some things, it is certainly not true for everything (there are far too many other factors involved for there to be any one perfect number).

Track (or tracking): Any analysis that measures how visitors or prospects go from interested to customer, and includes all the steps they took to get there (e.g., from seeing an ad somewhere, to visiting pages on a website, to hitting a Buy Now button) is called tracking. Analysts and copywriters use these tracking conversion analytics to test out different aspects of their marketing to try to improve results (see Split testing).

Typos: Any spelling or other grammatical errors found in copy.

U

Upsell: Any product offered after an initial sale that is related to the product being sold. In the internet marketing industry (IM) these items usually cost more (either as a one-off, or in some kind of continuity program). In the normal business world, an upsell can be both at a higher or lower price (e.g., "would you like fries with that?").

Unique selling point/proposition (USP). In order to stand out from the crowd, every product or service needs a USP. For example, Dyson's cyclone technology put it ahead of the vacuum market. See FAB.

V

Value: The most underrated attribute in copywriting. There is price and there is value. They are not the same thing. If we value something enough, we will pay all we have (or even borrow) to get it. Value is added by adding more things the buyer wants. That might include guarantees and extras as well as features other products don't have. The higher the perceived value, the easier the sale. If something has no value (to the prospect) you won't even be able to give it away.

Video sales letter (VSL): Take a sales letter and divide it into separate sentences. Create a slide for each sentence using presentation software (e.g., Microsoft PowerPoint or Apple's Keynote). Then video the slide show as you narrate over each sentence. The completed video is a VSL. They work because they're simple and take advantage of video plus fast moving frames.

W

White paper: Any content that is specifically about a product or idea in terms of features rather than benefits, and does so using scientific or industry-based language (often in the form of some kind of report) can be referred to as a 'white paper'. White papers are often used as part of a marketing campaign.